A JOURNEY OF DISCOVERY

Monroe County Outdoors

Terry W. Johnson

ISBN: 1535053429
ISBN 13: 9781535053426

To Donna, Angela, and Anna
Sharing our love and respect for the natural world
has made my life so much richer

CONTENTS

ACKNOWLEDGEMENTS

I want to thank Michelle McLaurin for editing the manuscript. Her thoughtful criticism, suggestions, and encouragement have made this volume the best that it can be.

I also want to thank Jackson Daniel for providing me with the opportunity to write my first column, which started me on a rewarding journey that has lasted more than a quarter century.

INTRODUCTION

I am a lucky man. For more than a quarter century, I have had the pleasure of writing a weekly column entitled Monroe County Outdoors for the *Monroe County Reporter*. This has enabled me to share with my readers my passion for the outdoors and the plants and animals that live there.

It is safe to say that nature is ingrained in the fabric of life in Monroe County. While the county is rapidly growing, it remains predominantly rural. Consequently, wildlife is all around those of us who live here. We see it in our backyards, as we drive to work, and to the grocery store. In addition, we do not have to leave the county to enjoy some of the best hunting, fishing, and wildlife watching found anywhere in Georgia.

Realizing this, over the years I have written stories about a wide range of outdoor subjects such as columns advising on the best times and places to enjoy outdoor recreation, telling the fascinating life histories of the plants and animals found locally, and offering tips on how to enhance the populations of these plants and animals.

Although I have personally met but a fraction of the people who read Monroe County Outdoors, it is difficult not to feel a kinship with those who week in and week out tote the *Monroe County Reporter* into their homes, open the paper to my column, and then take the time to read it.

The greatest reward I have received for writing the column has come when people have taken the time to let me know how much they enjoy it. Often I am told that a particular column reminded them of their childhood, their father, or their mother. Others have said that Monroe County Outdoors is the first thing they read in each edition of the paper each week. Some readers tell me they clip columns and send them to friends and relatives who live elsewhere in Georgia or in other states. Other readers have told me they save the columns they enjoyed in a notebook or pressed between the pages of books. Many of you have suggested that I publish a collection of these writings.

With this in mind, I have revisited the more than thirteen hundred Monroe County Outdoors columns I have written and selected a collection of articles that I hope will be of interest to as many of you as possible. Deciding which columns to include was a difficult task. I hope that I have included some of your personal favorites.

For those of you who have read these columns before and to those who are reading them for the first time, I hope you will enjoy them as much as I enjoyed writing them.

PART 1

Birds

AMERICA'S LONG LOVE AFFAIR
WITH THE HUMMINGBIRD

We Americans have harbored a long-standing love affair with the ruby-throated hummingbird. This affection is so widespread that I would say without hesitation that this feathered sprite is the most popular bird in Georgia.

With that in mind, I have often wondered just how long we have been enamored with this flying dynamo.

Recently I stumbled across a book written before the American Revolution that indicates our affection for the ruby-throated hummingbird is a lot older than I imagined.

The text entitled *Travels in America* was penned by an early Swedish-Finnish explorer named Peter Kalm and was first published in three volumes between 1753 and 1761. The English version was printed in 1770.

Peter Kalm was sent to colonial America by the Swedish Academy of Science to find plants and trees that could be used in Sweden to produce more food as well as fodder for livestock. Since the Swedes were also interested in developing a silk industry, Kalm was charged with trying to find mulberries that would grow in the cold Scandinavian climate. He arrived in North America in 1748 and made Raccoon (part of the former Swedish colony of New Sweden), situated along the mid-Atlantic coast on the Delaware River in what became New Jersey and Delaware, his home base. From here, he ventured as far north as Lake Champlain and Canada and westward into what is now western Pennsylvania.

In his account of his three-year odyssey in North America, he wrote a description of the ruby-throated hummingbird. Kalm called the bird simply "the hummingbird"; however, he noted that Swedish and English colonists called it "the king's bird."

He described it as being a little larger than a bumblebee, going on to say that while the bird fed, it made a beelike humming sound.

Kalm believed that the only thing hummingbirds ate was nectar, which he stated they sucked out of flowers through their long bills. In fact, he went on to say that nobody had ever seen the bird eat insects or plant juices.

We now know that hummingbirds eat both of these and that insects are an important food item for them. In addition, hummingbirds don't suck nectar from flowers with a straw-like bill. Instead, they lick the nectar out of blossoms using their long, slender tongue. A hummingbird can lick nectar out of a flower at a rate of roughly thirteen licks per second. The nectar moves up the tongue through a slender trough by means of a process known as capillary action and is drawn into the body when the tongue is withdrawn.

Kalm noted that hummingbirds visited a number of different kinds of flowers, particularly those with long tubes. He found that two of their favorites were bee balm and impatiens. Interestingly, both these plants are planted by hummingbird fanciers to this day.

His description of hummingbirds forcing half their body into particularly long, tube-shaped blooms was reminiscent of the times I have watched rubythroats nectaring at trumpet creeper flowers.

Surprisingly, he never mentioned the bird's preference for red flowers.

One of the most intriguing tidbits of information I gleaned from his work was that folks living in the country planted beds of all sorts of flowers around their homes. He wrote that such beds were popular with hummingbirds. However, if nearby windows were left open, hummingbirds would often chase one another through the open window and around the rooms of the house before zipping back out again.

Kalm seems to have been just as captivated with the birds" constant fighting as we are. He mentioned that if several hummingbirds tried to feed in the same bed, fights often broke out. Some of these encounters would be so violent that he was convinced they might end with one bird piercing another through with its long bill.

We now know that never happens. There is no way that the hummingbird's soft, pliable bill could pierce another bird.

I found his interpretation of what happens when a hummingbird tries to feed on a bloom that contains no nectar truly bizarre. According to Kalm, the bird would pluck the flower off the plant and throw it to the ground. He surmised this was the bird's way of never being fooled by the flower again. He went on to say that the ground in some gardens was at times blanketed with blooms, dislodged by hungry hummingbirds.

Kalm was aware that hummingbirds migrated. He wrote that with the approach of winter, the birds departed to "southern countries of America," only to return in the spring. In fact, he mentioned that one year he saw his first hummingbird on April 26 and that this was the first seen in the community that year.

He also mentioned that people would capture hummingbirds and keep them in cages. Most of these birds would die. However, he knew of one man who successfully kept a bird for several weeks, feeding it sugar water.

Like us, Kalm was struck with the bird's tameness. He mentioned that while they were feeding, he could walk up to within two yards of them.

Thanks to the writings of Peter Kalm, we now know that ruby-throated hummingbirds were the backyard neighbors of early colonists. It is also clear that our love affair with this tiny jewel of a bird has been going for more than 260 years.

If that isn't true love, I don't know what is.

A SPECIAL ARRIVAL

The arrival of the first hummingbird of the year is a special event. However, for Monroe County resident Debbie Menard, the appearance of the first hummingbird at her feeder this year was truly unforgettable.

The disappearance of ruby-throated hummingbirds in late summer and their miraculous reappearance the following spring has long been the stuff legends are made of. For example, the *Pennsylvania Cyclopedia* published in 1651 had a unique explanation for this phenomenon. The writer explained that when the flowers fade at the end of the summer, hummingbirds simply drive their bills into tree trunks. Here they remain until they are stirred back to life by spring rains.

We now know that rubythroats migrate to and from their breeding grounds in eastern North America to southern Mexico and Central America. However, to this day, many believe that such a tiny bird cannot make this journey on its own. Consequently, it supposedly hitches a ride on the back of a Canada goose. While such fanciful explanations are fascinating, how the birds actually accomplish this feat is every bit as astounding.

Each ruby-throated hummingbird that calls Monroe County its summer home makes a solo flight across the Gulf of Mexico in both spring and fall. Using only three-fortieths of an ounce of fuel, the tiny bird beats its wings about 2.7 million times crossing this broad expanse of water during a flight that lasts roughly twenty hours. Upon reaching land, the bird often returns to the same backyard it inhabited the previous summer.

Once it reaches the shore of the United States, it gorges itself on nectar and insects before heading farther north. How fast it migrates northward is affected by weather. Hummingbirds don't like to fly into strong headwinds. In fact, a hummingbird trying to fly into the teeth of a twenty-mile-per-hour wind will actually be forced backward.

Temperature also plays a key role in the bird's progress northward. Ruby-throated hummingbirds tend to follow the thirty-five-degree-Fahrenheit isotherm (average nightly temperature) northward. As a result, a colder-than-normal spring can dramatically delay migration. Conversely, during a warm spring, rubythroats move northward earlier than normal.

I received the first report of a ruby-throated hummingbird on March 3. The bird showed up at a feeder in extreme southwest Georgia at the Bainbridge home of Oscar and Bobbie Dewberry.

The earliest I have ever seen a ruby-throated hummingbird at my feeder is March 18. Last year, my wife and I didn't see a hummer at our home until March 27. Ken VanHoy reported the first arrival of a rubythroat in Monroe County in 2007. He saw one drinking at a feeder at the Nongame-Endangered Wildlife Program office on March 19.

This year Debbie Menard spotted and reported Monroe County's first ruby-throated hummingbird of the year on Saturday,

March 15. The sighting was a full nine days earlier than the first rubythroat made an appearance at her feeder last year.

March 15 was a very emotional day for Debbie. That was the day one of her closest friends was buried. This special lady knew how much hummingbirds meant to Debbie and would always bring her back a hummingbird-related gift whenever she returned from a trip. As Debbie drove home after saying good-bye to her dear friend, she thought to herself, "Wouldn't it be great if I saw my first hummingbird today? It would be a sign that she is in heaven and knows how much she meant to me."

Upon returning to her home, Debbie looked out at a feeder she had hung in her yard throughout the winter in hopes that it would attract a wintering hummingbird. During that time, both she and her husband, Ron, had gazed at the feeder hundreds of times. Not once did they see a hummingbird. However, this time was different—as if by magic, a male ruby-throated hummingbird suddenly appeared and began drinking the sugar-rich nectar that had been waiting for him. Debbie is convinced that the miraculous appearance of one of nature's most beautiful birds was no chance encounter. It was a sign that her friend had indeed gone on to a better place.

Debbie is also comforted to know that the hummingbird season has arrived and that scores of rubythroats will provide her and her husband hours of pleasure during the next several months.

If you haven't put up your feeder yet, do so soon. The last thing you want to see is a hummingbird hovering outside your kitchen window, looking for the feeder that had hung at that location the previous year. Although the arrival of the first hummingbird of the year in your backyard probably won't be as timely as Debbie Menard's, I know it will still be a special event.

HUMMINGBIRDS ARE COMING—DON'T BE LATE!

March is an exciting month. It marks the end of winter, and it is the month when ruby-throated hummingbirds begin arriving in Monroe County backyards. In spite of the fact that we all know this, when rubythroats begin arriving in our backyards, we are often late hanging out our hummingbird feeders.

Time and time again, people have told me that their first inkling that the hummers were back occurred when they looked out their windows on a cool March morning and spotted a male ruby-throat hovering where a feeder had been hung the previous year. Now that can really make you feel bad! If you don't want to go on that guilt trip, make it a point to put up your feeder right now, before you forget about it.

The earliest I have personally ever seen a hummingbird in my backyard is March 18. On that date in 2009, I spotted one visiting flowers on my blueberry bushes. The following Saturday, my daughter sighted two males fighting over a feeder in my yard.

Last year, Debbie Menard reported that she saw a humming-bird on Sunday, March 23. In 2008, she caught a glimpse of her first rubythroat of the year on March 15.

The first ruby-throated hummingbirds to arrive are males. Consequently, if you see one in mid-March, it is likely to be a male. Females show up about a week or two later. Therefore, if you don't spot your first hummingbird until April, it might be a female.

Food is always at a premium when the early arrivals wing their way into our backyards. However, unless the weather changes for the better really soon, the tiny birds will find nectar, their prima-ry food, especially hard to come by. This is because nectar-laden flowers seem to be slow to bloom this year. As a result, this year, feeders may be more important to early-arriving birds than they would be in a normal year.

With that in mind, make sure you have at least one humming-bird feeder in place when the birds arrive. Since hummingbirds are scarce in March, you don't need to fill feeders more than half full until more birds arrive.

Should you want to be the first in your neighborhood to attract a squadron of hummingbirds, there are a few things that you might try. For example, if not much is blooming in the yard this time of the year, consider tying pieces of red flagging tape or ribbons to barren bushes scattered around the yard. Supposedly, humming-birds passing by will mistake the strips of red material for flowers and drop in to take a look. Although they quickly discover the red markers don't offer any food, they soon turn their attention to your feeders and often stay for a while.

If you want to really think outside the box, place a red traffic cone atop your house. This might alienate your neighbors, but if you are a real hummingbird aficionado, you might think the risk is worth it.

You might also consider hanging multiple feeders around the yard. An abundance of food is always a magnet to ruby-throated hummingbirds.

One of the best things you can do is plant a variety of late-winter/early-spring bloomers that produce an abundance of nectar. I wish I could tell you that forsythia is such a plant, but I can't. Although it is showy and the namesake of our popular March festival, forsythia isn't a great nectar plant. Some of the plants that do fit the bill are yellow jasmine, crossvine, redbud, blueberry, Cherokee plum, and apple, to name a few.

One of the main sources of food for the first ruby-throated hummingbirds arriving in middle Georgia is tree sap provided by a woodpecker known as the yellow-bellied sapsucker. Consequently, look for active sapsucker holes in the trunks of the trees in your yard. These holes are often excavated in a circle around the trunks of trees. Sapsuckers peck these shallow holes into live trees to provide themselves with a dependable source of food. When the sugary sap wells up in these tiny "feeders," the sapsucker licks it up with the brushlike tip of its tongue. Hummingbirds, chickadees, butterflies, and other critters also dine on the sap. If you have fresh sapsucker holes on some trees in your yard, you are in luck. Rest assured that the hummingbirds will find them.

Let me know when you spot your first hummingbird. It will be interesting to see if the cold weather will delay their arrival. In the meantime, put up your feeder ASAP. I know you don't want a hummingbird to make you feel like a heel!

WHERE ARE THE HUMMINGBIRDS?

During the past few weeks, I have received a number of telephone calls and e-mails from Monroe Countians as well as folks living in such far-flung locales as Griffin, Macon, Butler, and Lincolnton. All have posed the same question: "Where are the hummingbirds?"

It seems that hummingbird feeders stocked with sugary nectar are going largely unused. Some homeowners report seeing only one or two hummers visiting their feeders. Others claim that the tiny birds have made a mass exodus and haven't visited their feeders in weeks. All fear the worst—something has decimated the beautiful flying jewels that provide these enthusiasts with hours of entertainment from spring until fall.

The truth of the matter is that nobody knows for sure what has happened to the birds. I have been studying hummingbirds for over two decades. Although I have learned much about hummingbirds during this time, with each passing year it becomes more evident that I still have much to learn about these fascinating birds.

This being said, I would like to offer my explanation for the apparent disappearance of the birds.

From late March and into April, the spring migration is in full swing. During this time, waves of northbound hummingbirds pass through our yards. Most stay only long enough to refuel before resuming their journey back to their breeding grounds. This is a grand time for hummingbird fanciers, as they will host more birds than they will during any other time of the year except from mid- to late summer.

The few male ruby-throated hummingbirds that stay behind set up breeding territories across the countryside. Each territory is roughly an acre in size, and each male vigorously defends this area from other males. However, he is more than willing to share his homestead with any female rubythroats that enter his domain. If you are lucky, your backyard will be situated in one of these territories. If it is, your feeders will typically be regularly visited by only one adult male and one or two females.

When the females begin nesting, they will spend upward of 80 percent of their time on the nest, incubating two tiny, black-eyed-pea-sized eggs. During incubation, they will make infrequent visits to your feeder, further reducing your chances of seeing them.

Another factor has come into play this year. The spring rains have helped Mother Nature produce more nectar-rich flowers than we have seen in years. Consequently, hummingbirds don't need to visit feeders as often as they might in drought conditions such as we have experienced during the spring for a number of years.

All of this is fixing to change. As soon as the females fledge their first broods, these young birds will begin showing up at your feeders. While the young females will look identical to their mothers, the adolescent males will look quite different. They will have rows of black spots running down their throats.

I promise you that the hummingbirds will return to your feeders, whether my explanation is correct or not. If 2009 proves to be like most years, you will see an explosion of hummingbirds by Independence Day. This marks the unofficial beginning of the summer hummingbird season. At this magical time of the year, if you have offered hummers a bounty of nectar plants and feeders, you will be rewarded with squadrons of hummingbirds zipping around your feeders. Meanwhile, I recommend that you maintain only a couple of feeders only partially filled with nectar until hummingbird numbers increase. This will cut down the amount of time you will have to spend maintaining your feeders, and you will save a little money on sugar.

I have long suspected that if we were to hold a contest to determine Georgia's favorite bird, the winner wouldn't be the bald eagle, wild turkey, quail, bluebird, or even our state bird, the brown thrasher. The ruby-throated hummingbird would win hands down. The outpouring of concern about the fate of the rubythroat during the past few weeks has convinced me that I am probably right.

FIGHTS BREAKING OUT
THROUGHOUT MONROE COUNTY

From dawn to dusk, countless fights have been taking place at homes throughout Monroe County. These altercations are not domestic disputes. Far from it. They are battles being waged by ruby-throated hummingbirds. Homeowners are reporting that the area around their hummingbird feeders resembles a war zone. Hummers are trying to knock one another off feeders or are engaged in aerial chases and dogfights for control of the airspace above our yards.

The ancient Aztecs believed that hummingbirds are resurrected warriors that have fallen in battle and have returned to wage war in the skies. Anybody that feeds hummingbirds will agree that this legend may indeed have merit.

I often hear people say, "I love my hummingbirds, but I wish they wouldn't fight so much. I'm afraid they are going to hurt themselves." Others say, "Those little birds are so mean!"

In truth, it is impossible to keep hummingbirds from fighting. It is as much a part of their nature as it is for mockingbirds to sing.

Also, don't be afraid that the birds will hurt themselves. They can't stab one another with their soft bills. The worst that can happen is flying into a window or latching onto one another and falling to the ground, where they become easy pickings for a cat or dog. Additionally, hummingbirds don't fight because they are mean. They scrap for two basic reasons—to defend a nesting territory or to defend a source of food.

Throughout much of the year, hummingbirds lead solitary lives. When males arrive in the spring, they quickly locate and defend a breeding territory that can range anywhere from one-quarter acre to a full acre in size. Whenever another male wanders into this domain, the male that has staked out this plot of ground will try to drive the interloper away. They will go so far as to attack artificial male rubythroats or even pictures of them! All of this is done in an attempt to eliminate competition for mates.

Male hummers don't restrict their aggression to other hummers. No indeed—they will routinely squabble with wasps, bumblebees, larger birds such as hawks, and even butterflies.

When the females arrive a few weeks later, the males try to woo these feathered beauties with courtship flights. If a female is favorably impressed with the male and the nesting sites he is defending, she will mate with him. However, until a female actually mates with the male, he won't share his stomping grounds with her.

Interestingly, once a female begins nesting, she turns the tables on him by driving him away from her tiny nest.

As spring wanes and summer begins, hummingbirds switch their attention to staking out feeding territories. That is what they are defending right now. The size of these areas varies widely depending on the number of flowers and the amount of nectar they produce. Some flowers produce four times or more nectar than others growing close by. The size of a feeding territory can change daily as certain plants cease flowering and others begin to bloom.

A backyard that is blessed with feeders and an abundance of flow-ering plants makes an ideal feeding area.

Right now, hummingbirds are trying to put on as much weight as they possibly can as they prepare to make their fall migration. Consequently, if a bird tries to defend too large an area, it will spend too much time chasing others away. Consequently, it can't store enough food to successfully make its rigorous migration. As a result, it will adjust the size of the area in which it feeds in an attempt arrive at a size that can be easily defended and provide it with enough food.

Here is an example of how this works. One researcher studied a rufous hummingbird that at first was defending a feeding area that contained 1,970 flowers. During that day, it only gained 0.15 grams of fat. The following day, it expanded its feeding territory to include 3,320 flowers and gained 0.25 grams of weight. On the third day, the rufous hummingbird defended a feeding area that contained only half as many flowers. However, this area allowed it to pack on 0.35 grams of fat.

The problem facing our local hummingbirds right now is that competition for food is at an all-time high. Not only do adults have to compete with young fledglings this year, they are also being in-undated with hummers raised in areas north of Monroe County. All are involved in a life-or-death struggle to store enough fuel to carry them across the Gulf of Mexico and on to the wintering grounds. For that reason, the number of hummingbirds visiting our backyards has increased dramatically, and the amount of time they spend feeding has also increased. This results in more fights breaking out around flower beds and feeders. It is not uncommon for Monroe Countians to feed one hundred or more humming-birds per day in August and early September.

Although you cannot stop rubythroats from fighting, there are a few things you can do to allow more hummingbirds to feed in your yard. Begin by putting out as many feeders as possible.

These feeders should either be located very close to one another or spaced widely apart. Some folks even arrange feeders at different elevations. In this way, you make it impossible for one or two dominant birds to keep all others from feeding.

I hope you will enjoy watching the action-packed battles being waged by these tiny feathered warriors during the next few weeks. If, however, you yearn for more violent action, you can always retreat to the living room and turn on the television.

June 30, 2010

HUMMINGBIRD NUMBERS EXPLODE IN JULY

Over the past several weeks, dozens of Monroe County hummingbird enthusiasts have asked me the same question: "Where are the hummingbirds?" I don't have an easy answer to this question. However, just as I know the nighttime skies will be illuminated with fireworks on the Fourth of July, I'm certain hummingbird numbers are soon going to explode in our backyards.

During the hummingbird migration in late March and April, thousands of the tiny birds arrived in Monroe County. Most of these long-distance migrants fed at our feeders and then continued northward to their breeding grounds. For other hummers, Monroe County marked the end of their spring migration. During this time of passage, many of us entertained as many as a dozen or more of these birds. However, when the migration was over, most folks found themselves feeding only one or two birds.

These birds remained here and nested. The males divided the county up into breeding territories of an acre or so in size. Within the unseen borders of each territory, the males tried to keep out other male hummingbirds and at the same time attempted to woo a mate. If your yard happened to be within such a territory, the male and its mate were probably the only hummers you saw visiting your feeders. Even then, you were more likely to see the male than its mate. This is because he doesn't share nesting duties with his mate and has little more to do than eat and keep interlopers away. Females were rarely spotted as they spent the vast majority of their time incubating two eggs the size of black-eyed peas.

During the past several weeks, they were joined at your feeders by the one or two young that fledged. Soon after the youngsters left the nest, each female laid a second clutch of eggs and began incubating all over again.

Once the Fourth of July rolls around, most of our local female rubythroats will be occupied with nesting duties. By the end of the month, most will have completed their 2010 nesting season. Consequently, we will soon be hosting a pair of hummingbirds and the offspring raised in two nesting attempts. In short order, they will be joined by birds preparing for or already migrating southward.

June 21 is an important day in the life of the ruby-throated hummingbird. This is the longest day of the year. Throughout the rest of the summer, each day thereafter will be a little shorter than the last well into winter.

The declining day length triggers chemical changes within their bodies. The tiny birds develop a seemingly insatiable appetite and go on a feeding binge. For the next several weeks, as they try to eat as much as they can, they get plumper every day. They are simply trying to store enough fuel, stored as fat, to make their fall migration.

Consequently, they will be visiting your feeders and flowers more often. A hummingbird might collect nectar from upward of fifteen hundred flowers in a single day. Our feeders are favorite feeding spots because the birds can easily drink a lot of nectar without much effort.

These birds will be joined by birds already en route to their wintering grounds. Rubythroats that breed along the northern fringes of the bird's breeding range begin their southward migration in early July. Consequently, they will add to the swelling numbers of hummingbirds congregating in your yard.

These numbers of hummingbirds that visit your yard begin rising around the Fourth of July and will peak from late August to early September. They then begin to wane until the last migrants leave by the end of October.

If you watch closely during the next two months, you will notice that the adult males will be the first to leave. They will eventually be followed by the females and immatures.

In the meantime, pull up a seat by your back window and enjoy the show. You are about to watch hummingbirds display their aerial skills as they hover, fly backward, and dive from upon high before pulling up just before crashing into the ground. Squadrons of the tiny aerialists will engage in countless dogfights as they vainly try to keep all other hummers from your feeders.

The Fourth of July fireworks shows might be louder and for a brief time more spectacular. However, the fact that the show staged by our ruby-throated hummingbirds will last from daylight to dark and go on for weeks is nothing to sneeze at.

When this scenario plays out, by summer's end you will wonder why you were so worried about the plight of these little birds a few months before.

HUMMINGBIRD MIGRATION
BEGINS IN YOUR OWN BACKYARD

For the past several weeks, hummingbird fanciers have enjoyed watching squadrons of ruby-throated hummingbirds displaying their aeronautical skills in their backyards. Across the state, these tiny dynamos have been flying between feeders and flowers, gorging themselves on sugar water and nectar. When they haven't been feeding, they seem to have been trying to keep others from enjoying the sweet bounty. While we have found their activities entertaining, to the hummingbirds, it has been a matter of life and death.

Hummingbirds don't simply show up at our feeders at this time of year by chance. Far from it. They converge on our backyards because they are preparing for their perilous fall migration or are stopping by to refuel as they head far to the south. Some ruby-throats that hail from the Midwest, the Northeast, and Canada actually begin their migration in early July. However, as far as we know, Georgia hummers commence their migration later in the summer.

The first birds to embark on this long journey are adult males. In the Peach State, most of them depart by the end of August. Females and those birds hatched this year follow later. By October, the vast majority of our hummingbirds have left for their winter homes.

The fall migration is triggered by declining day length. As the days grow shorter, chemical changes are triggered in the hummingbirds' bodies. These changes manifest themselves in the hummingbirds going on a feeding binge. In preparation for the journey, each bird must store the food needed to make this epic trip. This requires each bird to increases its body weight by two-thirds or more. This is the equivalent of a 170-pound man putting on an extra 85 pounds.

Ruby-throated hummingbirds can put on weight in a hurry. This is illustrated by the fact that during the summer of 1996, an immature hummingbird that I had banded and later recaptured increased its weight by 73 percent in just twenty-nine days.

The fuel for the fall migration is stored as fat. As the birds accumulate fat, they become so rotund that they aren't able to maneuver as easily as they could prior to their dramatic weight gain. If you were to hold one of these birds in your hand, it would feel like a bloated sponge.

We do not know how a hummingbird knows it is time to leave. However, when the time is right, it takes off and heads toward its wintering grounds in southern Mexico and Central America. Each bird travels alone. This means that a hummingbird hatched in the spring instinctively knows where it is headed. However, whatever path it chooses for its first migration appears to be the one it will use its entire life.

Unlike many migratory birds, ruby-throated hummingbirds seem to migrate principally during the day. The only exception seems to be when they are flying over the Gulf of Mexico. The length of this trip requires the birds to spend time flying in the dark.

Aside from this leg of the trip, a migrating rubythroat's day consists of refueling early in the morning, flying throughout most of the daylight hours, and then stopping in the late afternoon to feed until dark.

How long a bird remains at a stopover site, such as your backyard, depends on the weather and how much stored far it is carrying. Consequently, birds might stay upward of a week or more to replenish its fat reserves. Heavy rain and strong winds can delay migration. Wind direction also plays a key role in determining when and how far the birds migrate. Southbound migration seems heaviest when the birds can take advantage of a good tailwind.

The birds appear to migrate at a speed of approximately twenty-five miles per hour. While we don't know for sure at what altitude the birds travel, hot-air balloonists have seen rubythroats apparently migrating southward at altitudes of up to five hundred feet above the ground. This dramatically changes when the birds fly over the open Gulf of Mexico. Here, far from shore, southbound hummers have been spotted by fishermen and workers on oil and gas platforms winging their way along just above the waves.

Compared to some birds, the ruby-throated hummingbird's migration is a leisurely affair. It is thought that rubythroats migrate only about twenty-three miles a day.

Some ruby-throated hummingbirds reach their wintering grounds by flying overland down the Texas and Mexico coasts. However, most rubythroats raised in Georgia and elsewhere in the East fly across the Gulf of Mexico to reach their winter homes. The shortest distance across this broad expanse of water is approximately 500 miles. It is thought that such a flight takes a rubythroat 18 to 20 hours. To make such a flight, a hummingbird would have to beat its wings 2.7 million times, and to successfully complete it, each bird needs to carry at least three-fortieths of an ounce of fuel (fat). The larger females can carry enough fuel to make a 24.3-hour flight and can travel roughly 645 miles. Meanwhile, the males can carry enough fuel to stay aloft for 26 hours. This enables them to traverse some 604 miles.

If the birds encounter a tropical storm while over open water, they have little chance for survival. Even a strong headwind can be devastating. A hummingbird flying into a twenty-mile-per-hour wind will literally be pushed backward.

Each year, untold numbers of hummingbirds are lost in migration. The fact that the fall migration stretches over several weeks ensures that millions do make it.

As more and more natural stopover sites are destroyed each year, I am convinced that backyards festooned with feeders and flower beds ablaze with nectar plants will play an increasingly greater role in ensuring that hummingbirds will find enough food along their migration route. If you want to do your share to help the birds that bring you so much pleasure, make your backyard a haven for hummingbirds. Together, we can make a difference.

November 19, 2008

GEORGIA'S SECOND
HUMMINGBIRD SEASON

Now that November is here, more than likely you haven't seen a ruby-throated hummingbird in your backyard for quite some time. My wife and I were fortunate to see one as late as Halloween eve. However, since we haven't spotted one since, I guess it is safe to say that it too has departed on its epic flight to its wintering grounds across the Gulf of Mexico. I must admit that we were sad to see it leave. However, now that November has arrived, we are excited that Georgia's second hummingbird season is here.

During this special time of the year, we have a chance to host more different species of hummingbirds than at any other time. Georgia's second hummingbird season extends from November through February. While there aren't a lot of hummingbirds winging their way about the state during this four-month period, more different species of hummingbirds are seen in the Peach State than at any other time of the year. In fact, most of the hummingbirds seen during this, the coldest time of the year, are seen here only during these four months.

When the Nongame Endangered Wildlife Program (now known as the Nongame Wildlife Conservation Section) began re-searching hummingbirds in 1988, only two species of hummers were known to occur in the state. These were the ruby-throated and the rufous. One of the major reasons for this was that folks thought that most people took their hummingbird feeders down in September or October. This was done under the mistaken pop-ular belief that if they left their feeders up any longer, humming-birds would not migrate and then subsequently die with the onset of cold weather.

We now know that nothing could be further from the truth. You simply can't stop hummingbirds from migrating with food. If you stop and think about it, when the hummingbird numbers began to wane a few weeks ago, your feeders were brimming with sugar water and the flowers in your gardens were full of nectar and tiny insects. Yet in spite of this smorgasbord of sugary delights, the birds left.

Hummingbirds migrate in response to declining day length, not food abundance. As the days grow shorter, chemical changes take place in the tiny birds' bodies. This triggers the birds to go on a feeding binge. Their goal is to store as much fuel as possible to make their fall migration. This fuel is stored as fat. Each bird needs at least three-fortieths of an ounce of fat just to fuel its mi-gration across the Gulf of Mexico.

Concern for the birds' well-being during frigid weather was also unfounded. Hummingbirds can weather temperatures that dip into the teens and below. They accomplish this, in part, be-cause they can go into torpor. When in torpor, a hummingbird's heart and breathing rates and body temperature all drop dramati-cally. These dramatic changes reduce the amount of energy the birds needs to survive frigid temperatures.

Wintering hummingbirds eat a variety of foods. In addition to the sugar water we put out for them, they consume nectar found in winter-blooming flowers such as leatherleaf mahonia. On warm winter days, hummingbirds will also dine on small insects that periodically hatch throughout the winter months.

Another important source of food is provided by the yellow-bellied sapsucker. This unusual woodpecker is a winter resident throughout the state. It excavates tiny holes in living trees such as fruit trees, oaks, pecans, and others. When sap wells up in these holes, the sapsucker licks up the sweet fluid with the aid of a brush-like structure on the tip of its bill. Other animals, like butterflies, squirrels, Carolina chickadees, and hummingbirds, long ago discovered this source of food.

Once Nongame and other organizations got the word out that folks should keep at least one feeder out throughout the fall and winter months, the list of hummingbirds seen in Georgia began to lengthen.

While the ruby-throated is the only species of hummingbird known to nest in Georgia, it is rarely seen in most parts of Georgia during the winter. Most of the rubythroats that are spotted here in the winter are found along the coast and in the Thomasville area.

The rufous hummingbird holds the title of being the most commonly seen hummingbird throughout the winter here. This bird is no stranger to the cold. It nests as far north as southeastern Alaska. If you check a field guide, you will see that the vast majority of rufous hummingbirds winter in Mexico. However, for decades, increasingly greater numbers of these birds have been seen wintering throughout the Southeast. Each year, upward of one hundred or more sightings of rufous hummingbirds are reported in Georgia alone.

The list of other hummingbirds that are seen from time to time during the winter includes the black-chinned, calliope, Anna's, Allen's, broad-tailed, broad-billed, magnificent, buff-bellied, and green-breasted mango. Most of these birds breed in the American West.

A twelfth species, the green violetear hummingbird, has been reported here several times during the late summer. To date, though, since it hasn't been photographed or otherwise documented, the Georgia Ornithological Society has not placed it on the official list of birds found in the Peach State.

The best way for you to spot a wintering hummingbird is to leave at least one feeder up throughout the winter. Fill it about half full of nectar, and then sit back and wait.

Wintering hummingbirds can show up anytime throughout the second hummingbird season. When a bird does appear, there is no way to predict how long it will stay. Some are only seen a time or two while others linger for a few days or weeks. In some instances, they remain until spring. In addition, some birds return to the same backyard or neighborhood year after year.

Trying to attract a wintering hummingbird is much like playing the lottery. Chances are you won't have a hummingbird show up outside your back door. However, if one does, you are indeed very lucky and in for a real treat.

January 20, 2010

WINTER HUMMINGBIRDS

O ne of our favorite winter pastimes is bird feeding. For most folks, this means keeping backyard bird feeders stocked with a supply of seeds and suet. However, a few Monroe Countians maintain a hummingbird feeder supplied with fresh sugar water. Surprised? You shouldn't be, when you consider that eleven of the twelve species of hummingbirds that have been seen in the state have visited Peach State feeders in the winter. In comparison, only three species are known to occur here in the spring and summer.

The ruby-throated hummingbird is the only species of hummingbird known to nest east of the Mississippi River. Throughout the spring and summer, these tiny birds entertain us with their aerial acrobatics and iridescent beauty. It is far and away the most common hummingbird seen locally during these two seasons. By the end of October, all but a handful of these beautiful birds will have departed for their wintering grounds in southern Mexico and Central America.

In August, the vanguard of a flight of rufous hummingbirds begins arriving in Georgia. These birds will winter somewhere in the Southeast.

On rare occasions, green violet-ear hummingbirds are also sighted in the state. These large, predominantly green humming-birds call the mountain forests of southern Mexico and Central America their home. However, for some unknown reason, from mid- to late summer, some of the birds take flight and scatter throughout eastern North America, from Ontario to Georgia and other states of the Southeast. These elusive travelers rarely stay long at a feeder before moving on.

We are now in what I refer to as the second hummingbird season, which extends from November through February. During this four-month period, very few hummingbirds are wintering in Georgia. However, the list of hummers found here is impressive and, in addition to the ruby-throated, includes the rufous, black-chinned, calliope, broad-billed, broad-tailed, magnificent, buff-bellied, Anna's, Allen's, and green-breasted mango. With the exception of the green-breasted mango, which lives in Mexico and northern South America, all breed in the western United States.

By far the most common of our winter hummingbird visitors is the rufous. This sprite nests in the Pacific Northwest northward to southern Alaska. Each year, anywhere from fifty to more than one hundred of these tiny, long-distance migrants are seen in Georgia. In fact, chances are that if you see a hummingbird at your feeder during our second hummingbird season, it is probably a rufous.

These rare visitors to our state have undoubtedly benefited from more and more Georgians putting up feeders during the winter. However, these birds don't rely solely on our hummingbird feeders for food. In a normal winter, they will also eat small, soft-bodied insects that emerge throughout this, our harshest season of the year. They will also use nectar from some of the flowers that bloom in winter. Some of the plants that are potential sources of nectar are henbit, winter honeysuckle, tea olive, and leatherleaf mahonia.

Their main source of food, though, is provided by a bird with the curious name of yellow-bellied sapsucker. This winter resident in Monroe County pecks holes in the bark of trees, such as pecans, pears, apples, and oaks, to name a few. Often, these holes are arranged in neat rings around the tree. Sap wells up in the sapsucker holes, and the yellow-bellied sapsucker feeds on this sap, licking it up with its brush-tipped tongue. Long ago, other birds such as chickadees and hummingbirds found the sugary sap to their liking and now regularly visit these tiny reservoirs of nourishing liquid.

If you would like to attract one of these rare western visitors, put out one feeder filled only about one quarter full. A mixture of one part sugar to four parts water will not freeze until the temperature dips below twenty-five degrees Fahrenheit. When the temperature plummets below this, as has been the case lately, take the feeder in at night, and return it first thing in the morning. If this is too much trouble, place an alligator-clip lamp close to the feeder, and turn on the light.

Trying to attract a wintering hummingbird is somewhat like playing the lottery. Chances are slim that you will do either. However, during the next six weeks, if look out your frosty kitchen window one morning and spot a hummingbird drinking at your feeder, you will indeed feel like a jackpot winner.

April 21, 2010

HUMMINGBIRD FEEDING MADE EASY

One thing I have learned studying hummingbirds for more than twenty years is that the folks who consistently host the most hummingbirds are those that provide these tiny dynamos with a wide variety of nectar-bearing plants *and* well-stocked, clean feeders. In this week's column, I will try to provide you with everything you need to know about hummingbird feeding.

A lady in Massachusetts is credited with being the first person to feed hummingbirds with a feeder during the early 1900s. Her feeder consisted of nothing more than a trumpet creeper blossom attached to a glass bottle filled with sugar water. She hung her creation near some flowers frequented by hummingbirds and then sat back and watched. It didn't take long before hummingbirds began visiting the feeder—and the rest is history.

Today, hummingbird fanciers use a wide array of hummingbird feeders that are on the market. Designs range from ornamental feeders that are truly works of art to nothing more than topless salt shakers hung on a wire. Some resemble flying saucers; others are egg shaped. A few come equipped with guards that keep bees and yellow jackets away from the nectar. Some sport perches; others don't. Why, you can even buy feeders that look like mixed drinks like martinis and daiquiris.

While they all attract hummingbirds, some are better at it than others. In my opinion, the very best feeders are those that can be easily cleaned. If you can't thoroughly clean dead insects, mold, and bacteria from a feeder, don't buy it.

I have another personal preference. I look for a feeder that is equipped with perches. It seems to me that a hummingbird that feeds while standing on a perch feeds longer than one that has to hover while feeding. This provides me with more time to watch the bird during its visit.

Another thing to look for in a feeder is whether the nectar contained in the feeder will easily slosh out when the feeder is blown by the wind. This is important, because sugar water that collects on the outside of a feeder will attract stinging insects and ants.

Hummingbirds don't care if you fill your feeder with store-bought or homemade nectar. However, nectar made at home is far less expensive than that purchased in a store. Consequently, if you feed swarms of hummingbirds, you might want to use homemade nectar. This will save you a lot of dough.

If you want to make your own food, mix one part cane sugar with four parts water. Begin by bringing the water to a rapid boil, and then add the sugar. Boil the mixture for two to three minutes. This will kill most bacteria and mold spores lurking in the food. Allow the liquid to cool before refilling your feeders. Refrigerate the excess for later use.

Years ago, a Forsyth merchant told me that a lady came into his store one day and told him that she fed more hummingbirds at her home than anybody else in her neighborhood. When he asked her the secret to her success, she looked furtively around the store to make sure nobody could hear her before revealing her secret. Finally convinced that nobody was listening, she whispered into his ear, "I add a little gin to my nectar." I definitely don't recommend that you try this. We sure don't need squadrons of drunken hummingbirds crashing into our windows!

Before putting up your first hummingbird feeder, you must decide whether or not to add red food coloring to the nectar you will use. Keep in mind that the nectar you pour into your feeders doesn't attract the birds. The birds are attracted to the red artificial flowers that adorn the feeder. Additionally, they don't seem to prefer red over clear nectar. Some folks like to use colored nectar because it allows them to more easily track its use from a distance.

Although boiling hummingbird nectar will retard spoilage, bacteria and mold will eventually cause the fluid to sour. When nectar gets cloudy or when black patches appear on the inside of a feeder, you have problems. In the summer, this can take as little as three to four days. With that in mind, it is best to refresh nectar before it spoils. Tainted food can actually kill hummingbirds.

A lady once told me that she had a simple way of checking the fluid in her feeders—she simply tasted the sugar water every day. When it tasted sour, she knew it was time to change it. Hmm…not a very safe technique, but it worked for her.

Hang feeders where you can easily watch the comings and goings of these feathered dynamos. Keep in mind, though, that the food in feeders hung in the sun will sour before that contained in feeders hung in the shade.

I'm often asked if it is possible to stop hummingbirds from fighting over feeders. In short, you can't. Hummingbirds are highly territorial. As such, they are often reluctant to share food with other hummers, and some consequently spend most of their day fighting off others that want to dine at "their" feeders.

When I began studying hummingbirds, most folks took down their feeders in September and October. This was done due to the widespread belief that if they didn't, they would entice hummingbirds not to migrate. This would result in the birds perishing at the onset of winter.

Nothing could be further from the truth. Hummingbirds migrate in response to declining day length, not food availability. As summer wanes, hummingbirds begin storing the needed fat to fuel their long migration to their wintering grounds.

Incidentally, if you leave at least one feeder up throughout the fall and winter, you will have a chance of attracting one of the ten species of hummingbirds that are only seen in the Peach State in winter.

Well, that's all there is to it. If you try these tips, I am certain you will enjoy a great spring and summer watching hummingbirds patrol your yard.

COUNTING HUMMINGBIRDS IS
NO EASY TASK

August is indeed a special month. For the state's students, it marks the end of summer vacation and the return to the classroom. For Georgia sportswomen and men, the hunting season is ushered in with the opening of squirrel season. And for the backyard naturalist, August is truly the month of the hummingbird. Indeed, more hummingbirds visit Georgia backyards this month than at any other time of the year. During the hot, sultry days of August, it is not uncommon for some homeowners to host one hundred or more hummingbirds in a single day.

Whenever you have the pleasure of watching so many hummingbirds at one time, it is only human nature to wonder how many of the tiny birds you are actually looking at. However, if ever you try to count them, you quickly discover that this is no easy task. It seems almost like trying to count the stars in the sky.

Well, I am here to tell you that trying to estimate hummingbirds is a problem that has perplexed wildlife watchers and biologists for years. Although nobody has been able to devise a foolproof census technique, a couple of methods have been developed that offer fairly reliable estimates.

A little more than a decade and a half ago, an Arizona hummingbird enthusiast named Stephen Russell came up with a novel way to estimate hummingbird numbers based on how much food they consume. It stands to reason that the more hummingbirds that visit your feeders, the more food they eat. Right? Yes, that's true, but so many variables can affect food consumption, such as weather, size of the bird, and food availability, that you have to wonder how accurate population estimates that try to deal with so many variables are. Russell attempted to account for as many of these variables as possible. He began by weighing a gallon of nectar mixed at a ratio of one part sugar to four parts water (144 ounces). He then estimated the weight of the hummingbirds visiting his feeders. He also determined that his hummingbird feeders provided the hummingbirds visiting his backyard with 70 percent of their energy needs. He even went so far as to calculate that 14 percent of the nectar poured into his feeders was lost to evaporation, sloshed out in the wind, or consumed by ants, bees, yellow jackets—you name it. He plugged all of this information into a formula and came up with the estimate that a gallon of nectar mixed at the ratio of one part sugar to four parts water would feed 750 hummingbirds a day. To put it another way, a quart of this sugar-water solution fed some 187.5 birds a day.

Russell also determined that if hummingbirds rely totally on feeders, a gallon of the sugar nectar would feed only 549 birds. By the same token, a quart of this solution in this situation would feed 137.25 birds.

During his study, Russell found that during one hot August day when hummingbird numbers were at their peak, 8,980 hummingbirds fed in his backyard study area. He went on to estimate that during August (the month when hummingbirds were most abundant in his neck of the woods), 170,550 hummers dined at his feeders. Wow—and you thought *you* had some hummingbirds!

Anyway, if you know how much food you have placed in your feeders in the morning and compare it with what is left by the end of the day, you can use Russell's figures to estimate how many hummingbirds you host on a given day.

If this method requires too much time and effort, there are other ways to attack the problem. One such approach was shared with me by a hummingbird fancier several years ago. He told me that he counts the number of hummingbirds using his feeders by using his eyes like the shutter on a camera. He waits until hummingbirds are hovering all about his feeders. He then closes his eyes and counts the hummingbirds in the image portrayed in his memory.

I have tried this technique, and it simply won't work for me. Perhaps the hard drive in my head isn't large enough to handle a file that large. Who knows?

The technique that I recommend is also endorsed by the first lady of hummingbirds, Nancy Newfield. This Louisiana researcher and author has studied hummingbirds for more than thirty years. It is based on hummingbird banding studies. These studies compared the number of banded birds to unbanded birds caught in a backyard during the peak of the hummingbird season. Keep in mind that this technique works only during the summer, when hummingbirds are most plentiful. This means that if you live in the Peach State, it will work right now. You simply wait until you think you are looking at the maximum number of hummingbirds using your feeders at one time. Quickly tally the birds you see, and multiply this number by six. This will provide you with an estimate as to how many different hummingbirds you are feeding during a single day.

For example, if you count 30 birds, you are actually feeding approximately 180 hungry hummers.

You might even calculate your backyard hummingbird numbers using both techniques. It would be interesting to know how they compare.

At any rate, regardless of how many hummingbirds are visiting your backyard feeders this August, enjoy them while you can. Come September, their numbers will rapidly dwindle, leaving you waiting for next August and a new explosion of hummingbirds.

CARDINAL WATCHING

The northern cardinal is one of our favorite birds. It is pleasing to the eye, an accomplished songster, and a bird that brightens Monroe County backyards throughout the year. The fact that the cardinal has been named the official state bird in seven states is a testimony to how much this bird is admired.

Humans have had a long-standing affection for the cardinal. The Cherokees believed that the cardinal was the daughter of the sun. When the first colonists arrived in the New World, they too were captivated with this beautiful bird. However, European settlers were so smitten by the bird that they almost loved it to death. Literally thousands of the birds were trapped and shipped back to Europe, where they were sold as Virginia nightingales. Later, thousands of cardinals were slaughtered simply because hat makers used their feathers to adorn women's hats. Fortunately, laws were eventually passed to protect the cardinal and other songbirds.

During the nineteenth century, the cardinal was considered primarily a bird of the South. However, a little over a century ago, the cardinal began expanding its range. Today you are apt to see one in Boston, Toronto, and New York. In fact, the cardinal now ranges over most of the eastern two-thirds of the United States and southern Canada.

Locally, there is no better time to enjoy cardinals than in winter. Although cardinals don't migrate like white-throated sparrows and juncos, chances are you will see more cardinals in your backyard during the winter than at any time of the year. This is because cardinals form small flocks during the winter and often descend on our backyards in search of food.

If you want to attract a lot of cardinals, keep your feeders stocked with black oil sunflower seeds. Although the colorful birds will eat other feeder offerings, there is no question that sunflower seeds are their preferred food. During midwinter, it is not unusual to see a dozen or more cardinals feeding on these oil-rich seeds at our feeders. I particularly enjoy watching cardinals feeding just before dark. At this magical time of day, they are some of the last birds to feed before darkness envelops the land. In this subdued light, the male's plumage seems to glow.

If you want to take cardinal watching to a whole new level, all you have to do is learn to recognize a few of the bird's fascinating mating rituals. Fortunately, you can do this from the comfort of your home as these are acted out in your own backyard. If you are interested, there is no better time to start than right now.

During the winter, male and female cardinals get along with one another while they are feeding—for the most part. However, sometimes when a female ventures a little too close to a feeding male, he will quickly chase her away.

As you continue to watch cardinals feed throughout winter, one day you might witness something extraordinary. In fact, it might surprise you so much that you will want to see it again before believing it. A male cardinal will pick up a seed and offer it to a female feeding nearby. A male sharing seeds with a female becomes more common in the spring and will actually continue into early summer. This is the first indication that the breeding season is just around the corner.

As any resident of Monroe County can attest, the cardinal has a beautiful song. Unlike many birds, both males and females are equally accomplished songsters. Once the winter flocks have disbanded, dispersing across the countryside and beginning to set up their breeding territories, it seems that we can hear a cardinal singing whenever we step out into the yard. What you perhaps didn't know is that mated pairs are engaging in what is called countersinging.

Each bird will perch at a different spot within their breeding territory. One bird will sing a phrase several times. Its mate will mimic the song note for note. Eventually, when the first bird alters its song, the new melody is quickly repeated by its mate. Fortunately for those of us that enjoy listening to the birds sing, this back-and-forth duet can go on for hours.

Since the ritual is also being practiced by cardinals occupying nearby territories, unless you take the time to spot the birds singing, you don't know if you are listening to a mated pair, two males, or two females. It is believed that this practice helps cement the bond between a male and female; it may perhaps even aid in defining their breeding territory.

Now comes the hard part. If you are really lucky, you might even see a pair of cardinals in what is called the lopsided pose. It is seen far less often than food sharing. Birds engaged in this behavior will lean their bodies one way and then another. This creates a swaying motion.

Believe me, when you begin noticing and understanding the birds' mating behaviors, cardinal watching will be even more fun than simply watching them bathe and eat. It goes to show you that we can enjoy these magnificent birds without resorting to imprisoning them in cages or wearing their feathers on our hats.

CHIPPING SPARROWS
ARE INTERESTING BACKYARD NEIGHBORS

A ctivity around my bird feeders has definitely been down this winter. However, there is one bird that visits my feeders every day—the chipping sparrow. In fact, it would be safe to say that if you feed birds mixed seed, this is probably the most common bird at your feeders.

Although the chipping sparrow has been seen by practically everyone in the county, most don't know its name. Most people simply call it a sparrow. In fact, if you were to travel to the other 158 counties in the state, you would find that few people know it by name there, either. This is unfortunate, as this unassuming bird is both a fascinating and valuable backyard neighbor.

While it is true that most sparrows do indeed look very much alike, it is easy to separate this five-inch bird from its relatives. Adult chipping sparrows have grayish-white breasts, a black line through their eyes, a white eyebrow line, and a rufous cap. The cap takes on an added luster during the breeding season. Immature chipping sparrows look like the adults, with the exception that they don a light crown stripe instead of a rufous cap.

The bird's call has been described as a soft mechanical trill that sounds something like a rapidly repeated *chippy-chippy-chippy*. During the breeding season, which begins in early April and peaks in May and June, the chipping sparrow sings incessantly. Beginning well before daylight and continuing throughout the day, a bird might sing 330 times per hour. In fact, it has been estimated that a chipping sparrow might sing a minimum of 200,000 times and easily twice that often during the breeding season.

The chipping sparrow is one bird that has undoubtedly benefitted by the changes we have made in the landscape. Originally a bird of open pine woodlands, this bird can be found in a variety of other places, such as along highways, in parks, and in suburban areas alike.

There was a time when folks called it the social bird because it was so often found living near people. It was also named the hair bird because, interestingly, some chipping-sparrow nests have been found to be woven entirely of long horsehairs. Nowadays, since horses have given way to cars as our main means of transportation, chipping-sparrow nests are more apt to be constructed of grasses. However, lacking a source of horsehair, they will sometimes incorporate hair from cows and deer in their nests.

The chipping sparrow has long been recognized as a natural insect-control agent. Although the bird is considered primarily a seedeater, it does eat insect pests. This is particularly true during the nesting season, when 93 percent if its diet is comprised of insects. Three-quarters of these insects are considered to be pests. One early naturalist watched a chipping sparrow gobble down fifty-four cankerworms in one sitting. This tiny bird is particularly fond of caterpillars that are covered with spines. They also eat grasshoppers, beetles, and other six-legged critters.

Remarkably, in spite of the fact that the chipping sparrow is currently so abundant, populations of the bird fell off abruptly when house sparrows increased in number during the latter part of the nineteenth century. Fortunately, in those areas where house sparrow populations have gone down, chipping sparrows have made a dramatic comeback.

If you would like to attract more chipping sparrows to your yard, all you have to do is feed them. They don't dine on sunflower seeds; however, they are particularly fond of both red and white millet. They will also dine on mealworms. I personally feed them white millet. Since the birds are ground feeders, you can scatter the seed directly on the ground. However, they will also eat seed placed in feeding trays or hopper feeders.

This is the best time of the year to get acquainted with the chipping sparrow. In winter, local chipping sparrows and their northern cousins form flocks of two hundred or more individual birds. As such, it is not uncommon to have thirty to one hundred, or even more, feeding in your yard at this time of year. With the onset of the breeding season, these flocks break up, and far fewer birds will be spotted around your home in spring and summer.

However, if you begin feeding chipping sparrows now, chances are some will return to your feeders next year. In the meantime, once you get to know the chipping sparrow, you will wonder why you didn't make the acquaintance of this tiny brown bird a long time ago.

BARBED-WIRE ROYALTY

The king is back. I have no idea how long he and his cohorts have been in the county. However, I first saw them on April 6. They were where I expected to find them—holding court, perched on strands of barbed wire strung along a large field in Brent.

This king is popularly known as the eastern kingbird. Some folks call this bird the bee martin or bee bird. These names were given to the bird in the mistaken belief that it consumes large numbers of honeybees. A study conducted several years ago proved this reputation to be undeserved. The stomach contents of hundreds of eastern kingbirds were carefully analyzed. When all was said and done, only fourteen drone honeybees were found to have been taken by the birds studied.

While summering in Monroe County, eastern kingbirds prefer to dine on a wide variety of insects, such as leafhoppers, grasshoppers, flies, wasps, and beetles. Occasionally the birds will vary their diet by eating berries.

The eastern kingbird is what biologists call a sit-and-wait predator. It sits on a perch such as a tree, fence, or utility line and flies out and grabs an unsuspecting insect that ventures too close.

The bird's scientific name, *Tyrannus tyrannus*, would suggest that the eastern kingbird is a tyrant wherever it lays claim to a patch of the landscape. The bird has arguably come by this name honestly. The eastern kingbird will fearlessly defend its nest and young, commonly attacking both crows and hawks that venture too near its domain. Invariably, the kingbird will strike at these much larger birds from above and behind. While in many cases the kingbird never actually makes contact with the interloper, it has been known to literally latch on to the back of a hawk and peck at the raptor's head as it tries to escape.

The bird's aerial courtship is something to behold. The male eastern kingbird will fly up and down, zigzag back and forth, and make backward somersaults.

Eastern kingbirds are found throughout the state, preferring to nest and feed along the borders of woodlands and open fields, golf courses, farms, and open roadsides. Here, it builds its nest in a tree anywhere from two to sixty feet above the ground. Nests are typically located on the outermost ends of branches.

The bird's name suggests that its nest would be befitting a king. In truth, it is a large, bulky, rather unattractive structure made of weed stalks and coarse grass. It is lined with soft down collected from plants, fine grasses, and occasionally hair.

In this nest, the female lays two to five (typically three to four) eggs. While they may not match the exquisite beauty of the famous, delicately crafted Fabergé eggs, they are truly works of art in their own right. They are creamy white and adorned with irregularly shaped lavender, black, and brown blotches.

Should a brown-headed cowbird lay an egg in an eastern kingbird's nest, the female kingbird will unceremoniously toss it out.

In comparison, far too many songbirds incubate cowbird eggs and end up raising a cowbird at the expense of their own young.

While the eastern kingbird has no tolerance for crows and hawks, it will sometimes nest close to other birds. Orchard orioles, for example, will often nest in the same tree as an eastern kingbird. In one instance, an American robin nested within fourteen inches of an eastern kingbird's nest. Yellow warblers and Baltimore orioles have also been found nesting close to eastern kingbirds.

The eastern kingbird is not blessed with ornate plumage. Its trappings are of a more stately nature. Its head, back, tail, and wings are black while its underside is white. Its tail is also tipped in white, and a red "crown" adorns its head. However, this adornment is rarely seen. It is usually displayed only when the bird is agitated or defending its nest.

When residing in its summer realm, the eastern kingbird lets both man and beast know that it is holding court. While a European king uses brass horns to make such announcements, the kingbird prefers to noisily call *kit-kit-kitter-kitter* throughout the day. In fact, you often hear the bird long before you spot it. The calling is often accompanied by short flights punctuated with fluttering wing beats.

By early September, the king is ready to depart for its winter home in South America. In fact, you would be hard pressed to find an eastern kingbird when October rolls around.

When you see eastern kingbirds forming flocks, you know that they are ready to abandon their summer kingdoms. These flocks can number from a few dozen upward to half a million birds.

When it come time to leave the county, the bird's diet begins to change. While insects are still a staple, the bird augments its diet with pokeberries and other wild berries.

Eastern kingbird populations have demonstrated a slow but steady decline over the past four decades. Although the reasons for this downward trend are not fully understood, biologists believe that loss of habitat both here and in the wintering grounds as well as pesticides are key suspects.

I for one hope the reign of our barbed-wire royalty will not come to an end. If it does, we will have lost an irreplaceable treasure that is worth more than a king's ransom

July 29, 2009

PURPLE MARTINS ARE LEAVING

The purple martin is one of our most beloved birds. It is also one of our first migratory breeding birds to arrive in the spring and one of the first to leave on its fall migration. In fact, these birds are in the process of leaving now.

The purple martin has a long association with humans. When the first European settlers arrived in what is now the southeastern United States, they found that gourds, sometimes called calabashes, were hung near many Native American villages. The gourds were hung close by the encampments in an attempt to attract nesting purple martins. They knew that nesting martins would vigorously defend their nest sites from any bird perceived to be a threat to their eggs or young. By so doing, these large swallows would inadvertently help keep crows, vultures, and hawks from the drying meat and hides that were hung near the gourds used by the birds.

The new settlers were quick to adopt this practice and erected gourds and later other nesting structures around their own homes. The famous naturalist and painter John James Audubon noted in his journals that he could always tell the quality of a roadside tavern by the quality of the nest sites offered to the martins by the tavern's proprietors.

Purple martins on their spring migration arrive in the Peach State as early as February. After what seems an all-too-brief time, the majority of the birds leave in late July and early August. It is unusual to see a purple martin here after September 1. However, some can be found in Florida as late as October.

My granddaughter and I saw both adult and young purple martins at Dauset Trails two weeks ago. However, many martins have already embarked on their fall migration.

You can always tell when purple martins are getting ready to depart—they gather together in large flocks. Some of these flocks are extremely large, numbering anywhere from one hundred thousand to half a million birds. About an hour before dark, the birds form large flocks in spots known as preroosting areas. Then, just before the sun drops below the western horizon, they fly to their nighttime roosts. The flocks converging on these roosts are often so large that they can be picked up on radar.

You would think that the birds would remain at the nighttime roost until daylight; however, this is not the case. Typically, the birds leave the roost hours before dawn.

Biologists have long known that purple martins winter in the Amazon basin, in an expansive area encompassing both Brazil and Venezuela. However, the majority of the birds overwinter in the Amazon valley of Brazil.

Remarkably, until recently, little was known about the bird's migratory behavior. We knew that purple martins nesting in much of eastern North America migrated by day until they reached the Gulf of Mexico and then winged their way over five hundred or more miles of open water. This flight requires them to fly both day and night. Beyond that, we didn't even know something as basic as how long it took the birds to reach their destination. All of that changed two years ago.

Prior to the 2007 fall migration, researchers captured twenty purple martins in northwestern Pennsylvania and equipped them with miniature transmitters. This enabled biologists to track one of these birds as it made a 4,300-mile journey from Pennsylvania to Brazil. They found that the bird made the entire journey in forty-three days.

One of the things biologists learned was that the bird made frequent stops along the way. In fact, when it reached Mexico's Yucatan Peninsula, it hung around for about four weeks.

What was even more remarkable was that the bird made its return flight home the following spring in less than two weeks. This meant that that this long-distant migrant made fewer stops while averaging an amazing 311 miles per day. This set the ornithological world on its heels, as the bird's spring migration was up to six times faster than the experts had thought.

If you would like to observe martins congregated at a large roost, one of the best places to go is just south of Alabama's Wheeler Dam in north Alabama. Here, upward of five hundred thousand purple martins roost on a one-acre island in preparation for their fall migration. The birds can be viewed at a distance of only two hundred yards from a viewing area. For information on the status of the birds using the site, contact the Alabama Wildfire and Freshwater Fish Division (256-353-2634).

It will be a sight you will never forget.

BLACK BLUEBIRDS
AND OTHER BACKYARD ODDITIES

A long time ago, I learned that when it comes to wildlife, never say never. Over the years I have answered a lot of calls from folks reporting unusual things going on in their backyards. Now, I'm not talking about the behavior of their neighbors or little green men. What I am referring to are the sightings of rare animals or wildlife engaging in seemingly bizarre behavior.

For example, several years ago I received a call from a lady in Henry County. She wanted to know if it was unusual for a male bluebird to feed young Carolina chickadees. I told her that it most certainly was. I was so intrigued by her story that the next day I made the trek her Henry County home to see this strange behavior for myself.

When I arrived, the lady of the house led me into her backyard and pointed to the place where the chickadees were nesting—a red-ceramic nesting structure suspended from a pole. The young chickadees' parents made trip after trip to and from the box in what appeared to be a vain effort to satisfy the hunger of the tiny birds.

Every ten minutes or so, a male bluebird carrying food arrived at the opening to the nest site. In one instance, it brought a large walking stick. Needless to say, it had a lot of trouble maneuvering the long insect into the entrance hole. After several attempts, it succeeded, only to find the young chickadees apparently unable or unwilling to down the long walking stick.

In order to swallow this meal, a young chickadee would have to possess the talents of a sword swallower. Eventually, after failing to coax any of the nestlings to eat the supersized meal, it flew off, taking the walking stick with it. I am sure the youngsters were glad to see the bluebird leave.

A Monroe County resident shared with me a fascinating tale of a great blue heron dining on an unusual meal. The man's back-yard abutted a small lake frequented by a great blue heron. One day, as the man was enjoying his morning coffee, he watched the tall bird deliberately walk from the pond to his bird feeders lo-cated some forty to fifty feet away. Once there, it positioned itself near the feeders and stood motionless. In a few minutes, an east-ern chipmunk dashed up to fill its cheeks with sunflower seeds. Suddenly, without warning, the heron speared the chipmunk and swallowed the hapless animal head first. It then returned to the pond.

Carolina wrens are renowned for nesting in unusual places such as clothespin bags, shoes, old hats—you name it. Recently a Clarke County resident told me that Carolina wrens had nested on a shelf in her garage. Since they kept the garage door down throughout the day, she and her husband wondered how the tiny brown birds were able to enter the garage. Watching carefully, they finally learned the birds' secret: the wrens were entering and leaving the garage through the pet door at the base of the garage door.

I have been fortunate enough to see one albino bluebird in my life. This bird nested in a box along the edge of a front yard in Monroe County. While such a bird is a rare find indeed, it doesn't compare to a black bluebird. Consequently, when I got a call reporting such a bird nesting in a bird box in Carroll County, I didn't waste any time getting there. The bird was nesting in a blue bird box. That's right—these birds were nesting in box painted blue. At a distance, the bird appeared to be totally black; however, when I viewed the bird through binoculars, I could see streaks of blue feathers in its charcoal-colored plumage.

Rare birds show up in backyards quite often. A man in Houston County was surprised to find a black-headed grosbeak at his feeder.

One cold winter morning while my wife and daughter were looking out the dining room window, a yellow-headed blackbird landed on one of our feeders. Knowing that I desperately longed to see a yellow-headed blackbird, they immediately called the golf course to let me know that the rare bird was at my feeder. The man on duty at the pro shop ran out and caught me on the first tee before I hit my first drive. I convinced myself that the bird would still be there when I finished the round and went ahead and played eighteen holes. You guessed it—when I returned home, the bird had left. I have never lived that one down.

All of the rare hummingbirds documented in Georgia have been reported in backyards. For example, a broad-billed hummingbird showed up at a home in Macon. Once the report of the bird got out, folks from more than a dozen states flocked to Macon to see the bird. It didn't take Neighborhood Watch long to spring into action, and birders were soon confronted by Macon police officers asking what they were doing in this quiet, residential area.

The point I am trying to make is that you don't have to travel to the Galapagos Islands or the Grand Tetons to see something very special. Truly amazing things and sightings are made in Georgia backyards every year. However, if you don't spend a little time watching and listening, you will never know what you missed.

Once you have spotted something that seems out of the ordinary, let somebody in the Nongame Wildlife Conservation Section know about it. Don't assume that what you have seen is common. Who knows, you may spot a behavior never witnessed by biologists. Or it might be the first time that particular animal has ever been seen in that part of the state. Remarkably, little is known about the distribution of many species of wildlife in Georgia.

Summer is a great time to start spending more time watching the wildlife in your backyard. Once you begin spending a little more time watching your wildlife neighbors, you will be astounded by what is going on just outside your backdoor.

THE LONG PROCESSION

More than twenty species of ducks pass through Monroe County. Most of these birds are northern migrants and are only spotted here in the fall or winter. If they are, as some suggest, the royalty of the bird world, the vanguard of the annual fall royal procession will soon be reaching middle Georgia.

Each year, this parade is led by the blue-winged teal. It arrives weeks before many species of ducks have shown any inclination to migrate. In fact, some are winging their way toward their wintering grounds as you read this column. Remarkably, although they are the first to reach our county, they have perhaps the most complex migration pattern of any North American duck.

The center of the blue-winged teal's nesting grounds is the Prairie Pothole Region of the plains states and western Canada. Here, they breed along the edges of the small ponds that dot the vast grasslands of North America's most important waterfowl production area.

Most of these tiny ducks winter in the northern reaches of South America. However, some spend the winter months far south of the equator in Brazil and Peru. This earns the bluewing the added distinction of wintering the farthest south of any duck that breeds in North America.

One blue-winged teal banded in the western Canadian province of Manitoba was recovered near Lima, Peru, some 4,000 miles away. In another instance, a young bluewing banded in the Peace-Athabasca Delta of western Canada made it all the way to Maracaibo, Venezuela, approximately 3,800 miles away in only a month. This meant that this bird, on its first migration, averaged a flight of 125 miles per day.

However, the routes some of these birds take to get there is an even more remarkable story. It just so happens that while the blue-winged teal leads the waterfowl procession southward, it is one of the last ducks to return to its breeding grounds. In fact, many of these ducks don't begin the spring migration until March. When they finally arrive on the breeding grounds, ducks such as gadwalls, pintail, shovelers, and others have already begun their nesting chores. Then, in a few short weeks, they raise their young and are ready to take to the skies once again.

Drake bluewings are the first to depart. They gather up in small groups in places called staging areas. Depending on where they nest, bluewings use one of a dozen or more migration routes that various populations use to reach their wintering grounds. Many, for example, actually fly eastward in a path that takes them all the way to New Brunswick and Maine. Once there, they head out over the cold North Atlantic along a route that carries them to the West Indies and eventually South America.

Undoubtedly some of the birds that we see in Monroe County take a more southeasterly path that runs through middle Georgia and then on into Florida, the Bahamas, Cuba, and eventually South America.

The first bluewings reach the Peach State around the first week in August. These are flocks of males. As the summer wanes, the composition of the flocks changes. In fact, by the middle of September, most of the bluewings seen in this neck of the woods are adult females and their young.

The best places to look for them are on small bodies of water such as farm ponds. I have even seen them on the small pond in front of the eighth tee at the Forsyth Golf Course.

Bluewings are small. Drakes tip the scales at just over a pound and have wing spans of twenty-four inches. Female are slightly smaller. The adult males are unmistakable, sporting a white, crescent-shaped patch that extends all the way from the top of their heads to their chins. Additionally, the top leading edge of the males' wings are powder blue. These prominent blue patches catch your eye when the birds are in flight. Females are drab, the feathers cloaking their sides looking like large scales.

Although the blue-winged teal is an accomplished flyer, the speed of its flight has long been overestimated. The famous naturalist and painter John James Audubon likened the flight speed of the blue-winged teal to that of the passenger pigeon. In 1899, a sportsman wrote that bluewings can fly some 125 mph. Modern equipment has enabled biologists to more accurately measure the flight speed of this tiny duck to be a little over 50 mph.

Whether you are a sportsman or just simply enjoy the sight and sound of wildlife, I hope you will be lucky enough to spot a flock or two of bluewings during the next few weeks. If you don't, you can take heart knowing that in a couple of months, you will be able to see other ducks, such as American wigeon, lesser scaup, mallards, hooded mergansers, and a host of other members of the royal family. They will follow in an orderly, well-timed procession that has been passing this way for generations. Let's hope that it will continue for untold generations to come.

October 10, 2001

A BUFFET FOR WOOD DUCKS

Fall is a time of plenty for many wildlife species, particularly those that eat fruits, nuts, and berries. While most animals prefer certain foods, invariably their diet is as varied as the different kinds of animals that compete for these nutritious foods. Such is the case with the wood duck.

During the autumn, acorns are an extremely important part of the wood duck's diet. When acorns are available, they will sometimes make up 90 percent or more of their diet.   However, even then, wood ducks will consume a host of different kinds of small animals and other plant foods. This wild buffet ensures that the nutritional needs of Georgia's most abundant duck are met.

In the fall, it is common to find wood ducks slowly floating down lazy, tree-shrouded Piedmont streams. The ducks are drawn here by the acorns that rain into the water from willow, water, and other oak trees guarding the banks of these ribbons of water. The acorns of these willow and water oaks are often favored by wood ducks over all others. Since they are small, they are a snap for the ducks to swallow. In addition, their thin seed coats make them easy to digest.

Wood ducks will also eat other acorns. They are particularly fond of eating acorns produced by trees growing in the bottomlands surrounding rivers and streams. Here they will often venture far from water, walking along the forest floor in search of food.

Although cherrybark oaks produce far fewer acorns than willow or water oaks, they too are relished by wood ducks. Some food-habit studies have found that wood ducks prefer the acorns of the cherrybark oak three to one over those of the willow oak.

Both red and white oak acorns are consumed to a lesser extent. The acorns of the red oak are available to wood ducks much longer than are those of the white oak. White oak acorns germinate soon after they fall while red oak acorns persist into winter.

The seeds, fruits, and berries of a number of other trees and shrubs are important to wood ducks. You might be surprised to learn that wood ducks actually eat the hard nuts of hickories. They will also dine on such delicacies as pecans and dogwood berries and the seeds of hackberry, sweetgum tupelo, and buttonbush. Cypress cones and seeds are wood duck favorites a little farther south of Monroe County.

The seeds of a number of other plants are also important. Wood ducks devour the seeds of burrweed, spikerush, wild millet, and smartweed.

Asiatic dayflower is also a favorite where it is found. This plant grows in abundance in parts of South Carolina. Realizing its value as a wood duck food, hunters have introduced Asiatic dayflower in beaver ponds across the state. These sportsmen either transplant plants or scatter seeds taken from the crops of harvested woodies.

Corn and millet are among the most common cultivated grains eaten by wood ducks. The ducks will glean corn and millet from agricultural fields. However, locally, they most often feed on these crops in areas prepared especially for ducks. Corn is often planted in fields that are later flooded specifically to provide ideal feeding areas for woodies and other waterfowl. Japanese millet, on the other hand, is one of the few crops that can be planted on extremely wet soils. Consequently, Japanese millet can be scattered on the exposed mud bottoms of beaver ponds in late summer.

Typically, animals comprise 10 percent or less of the wood duck's fall diet. Insects are by far the most common animals consumed. Wood ducks eat leaf hoppers, squash bugs, grasshoppers, beetles, moths, flies (both adults and maggots), and water striders. Among the other animals devoured are spiders and Asiatic clams.

The value of bottomlands for wood ducks can't be overstated. Here, our most beautiful duck finds both nesting sites and feeding areas that provide it with the diversity of food items needed to balance its diet. These needs cannot be met with nest boxes and food plots alone. Sadly, we are losing these valuable wildlife areas at an alarming rate. Our ability to preserve and better manage those valuable bottomlands that remain will determine whether or not the wood duck will continue to thrive throughout the twentieth century.

February 10, 2011

PORTRAIT IN BLACK AND WHITE

During the next few weeks, many of the ducks that have wintered in Monroe County will be returning to their breeding grounds. Among them will be the northern shoveler, green-winged teal, gadwall, bufflehead, and American wigeon, to name a few. One of the first to leave is the hooded merganser. Although the vast majority of this, our smallest merganser, will leave the Peach State behind, every so often a pair lingers behind to nest in the Deep South.

Weighing only about one and a half pounds, the hooded merganser is just a tad smaller than the wood duck. Like the wood duck, it nests in natural cavities in trees as well as nesting boxes.

The populations of both species suffered tremendously from widespread loss of nesting habitat and overhunting during the nineteenth and early part of the twentieth centuries. Realizing the plight of these birds, hunters and other conservationists were able to persuade their elected officials to pass stringent hunting regulations to protect the birds. Meanwhile, the development of artificial nesting boxes helped offset the loss of natural nesting sites.

I begin spotting my first hooded mergansers from late October into November. Unlike many species of ducks, hooded mergansers don't migrate in large flocks. Typically, the birds travel alone, in pairs, or in small flocks numbering less than a dozen.

While hooded mergansers are with us, they can be seen in a variety of habitats. You are just as likely to see them feeding in small ponds within the city limits of Forsyth, relaxing on farm and beaver ponds, and floating down meandering woodland creeks as you are on High Falls Lake.

The male hooded merganser is among the most beautiful of all ducks. Some argue that it is more gorgeous than the wood duck. Predominantly black and white, its most striking feature is a fan-like crest displaying a large white patch bordered in black. Male hooded mergansers can raise and lower this crest at will. When it is closed, all that remains of the white patch is what appears to be a white bar.

While not as showy as the drake, hen hooded mergansers are attractive in their own right cloaked in their soft, reddish-brown feathers.

Drake buffleheads and hooded mergansers are often confused with one another. Actually, they are not that difficult to separate. Just remember that the white on the male hooded merganser's crest is always surrounded with black. In comparison, the white on the head of the bufflehead lacks a black border at the back of its head.

Unlike wood ducks, hooded mergansers dive for most of their food. High on their list of preferred items are small fish, aquatic insects, and other invertebrates such as crayfish. The tiny tooth-like structures on the bird's bill allows it to efficiently capture these small animals.

Local waterfowl hunters will tell you that these small ducks fly fast and straight and readily pitch into decoys. However, many wildfowlers—like me—don't shoot them. While far from being imperiled, it is far from being one of our most common ducks. Additionally, being a fish-eating duck, hooded mergansers often taste fishy.

The vast majority of hooded mergansers nest far north of Georgia. However, they nest in small numbers as far south as Florida. Hooded mergansers occasionally nest in our state. Although I have checked hundreds of wood duck nesting boxes, I have never been lucky enough to find one being used by a nesting hooded merganser. However, other biologists have discovered them nesting just across the river on the Piedmont National Wildlife Refuge. Additionally, a friend found a hen hooded merganser nesting in a wood duck box near Albany. That was noteworthy enough; however, what made this discovery even more remarkable was that the hen was trying to incubate her eggs while a gray rat snake was curled around them.

I hope you saw hooded mergansers this year. I was lucky enough to see them many times. My most memorable encounter with a hooded merganser took place on a winter afternoon. I just happened across a drake floating in the calm water of the waterfowl impoundment on the Rum Creek Wildlife Management Area. As the drake slowly swam away from me, it was closely followed by its equally impressive reflection in the mirrorlike water. This was indeed a portrait in black and white. It was an image I will never forget.

SPECTACULAR SANDHILL CRANES PASSING THROUGH TOWN

For well over two million years, a call that sounds like a rolling *agro-a-a-a* interlaced with a cacophony of shrill, almost bell-like rattles and croaks has been uttered high above Monroe County. It is a call that can be heard up to three miles away. The first humans to hear it here were Native Americans who lived along the Ocmulgee River and its tributaries. Later, the first European settlers listened to it as they tried to eke out a living from the red Monroe County soil, forests, and streams. For the past few weeks, folks throughout the county have stopped whatever they were doing and cast their eyes skyward when they too heard the call. They were listening to the strange vocalizations of the greater sandhill crane.

Let's take a moment and look at where the birds began their journey, where they are going, and how they will get there.

The birds passing over the county have been wintering anywhere from south Georgia to central Florida. Each year from mid-January to April (the peak migration takes place in February and March), they will take to the sky and embark on a long-distance trek that will carry them the length of Georgia along a broad pathway that extends from the southeast to northwest corners of the state. This brings the birds directly over middle Georgia. In fact, all of the sandhills that winter in Florida pass along this unseen aerial highway.

The birds' northward journey then takes them across the states of Tennessee and Kentucky and then on into the Midwest. There, they will scatter across their breeding grounds, which range from Michigan and Ohio to southern Ontario.

Typically, the birds begin their trip northward on a day with clear to partly cloudy skies and southeast winds. During migration, the birds begin their daily flights anywhere from an hour and a half to five hours after sunrise. Depending upon the weather and other factors, the large birds may fly from one to ten hours a day. This allows them to travel on an average 150 miles a day. However, on a good day, they may fly 500 miles or more before resting for the night. From time to time, they might even fly after the sun has set. However, more often than not, the birds are ready to land roughly two hours to a quarter of an hour before sunset.

Flight speeds vary from fifteen to a little more than fifty miles per hour. As might be expected, the direction and strength of the wind has a tremendous impact on the birds' flight speed and the distance they can cover. Rarely do they try to fly into a headwind.

Sandhill cranes fly at altitudes varying from five hundred to fifty-two hundred feet above the ground. However, throughout most of their northward migration, the birds are flying at altitudes ranging from five hundred to twenty-five hundred feet.

During migration, sandhill cranes travel by flapping their wings, spiraling, or soaring. Most of the time when we see the birds, they are flapping their wings and flying in an undulating *V* formation. This form of travel requires the most energy.

At other times, the birds are spiraling upward. In such cases, they are riding the winds that can reach ten miles per hour or more created by thermals (columns of warm, rising air). These columns of air can reach upward of five thousand to six thousand feet into the sky. You are most apt to see this behavior late in the morning and at midday when these updrafts are most common. The circular pattern of a flock follows the outer edge of the thermal. The draft created by the rising warm air allows the birds to reach great heights. Sandhill cranes riding thermals expend little energy to stay aloft. All they have to do to follow a thermal is occasionally flap their wings.

The same is true of cranes that glide. When gliding, they simply set their wings and soar along with the prevailing wind. It is not unusual for the cranes to glide for hours without ever flapping their wings.

Unfortunately, sandhill cranes rarely set down in our county for the night. When such an event does occur, it is usually the result of fog or storms that hinder their flight northward. When they alight, we can gain a better appreciation of their size. These are truly big birds. Males can weigh eleven to fifteen pounds while females tip the scales at a little less than nine pounds. Their wingspan is roughly seven feet, and they stand around five feet tall.

Throughout much of the first half of the twentieth century, greater sandhill cranes were persecuted. As this was the case, by 1940 wildlife biologists estimated that only one thousand of them remained in the wild. However, vigorous protection of the remaining birds coupled with habitat management has brought the birds back—to the point where it is estimated that one hundred thousand greater sandhill cranes ply our skies today.

This is great news for everyone who enjoys wildlife. The sandhill crane migration remains one of the most spectacular wildlife events found anywhere in the world today. For those of us who live in Monroe County, the return of the greater sandhill crane provides us with the opportunity to watch an epic wildlife migration without even having to leave to comfort of our own backyard. I think that is pretty neat! I hope you do too.

THE SKY DANCE

The sky dance is now being performed on a stage near you. This truly spectacular show combines the breathtaking elements of aerial acrobatics with lyrical song and dance. You won't find the production being put on at The Rose. This event is taking place on small stages scattered across the county. While far less well known than theatrical presentations such as *The Sound of Music* or *Oklahoma*, this three-act play is every bit as dramatic and compelling. It is the mating ritual of the American woodcock, commonly known as the timberdoodle.

The American woodcock is indeed a strange bird. While it is a shorebird, it is more at home is shrubby, moist woodlands than the shore. It is also a game bird that is twice the size of our prince of the game birds—the quail. The star of the show, the male woodcock, will never be accused of having the leading-man looks of a Cary Grant. It possesses a three-inch-long bill that it uses to probe soft soils for its favorite food—earthworms.

In addition, its eyes are set so far back that it can see around its entire body without ever moving its head. However, after seeing it perform, you will agree it gives an award-winning performance.

Locally, around the time we ring in the new year, woodcocks begin acting out the sky dance. The birds perform on small stages that are nothing more than bare spots or areas covered in short grass near woodlands. They will even use a dirt road as a singing ground. Unless the spot changes dramatically, the same singing grounds will be used year after year. In fact, chances are good that a male will return to the same stage the following year. While a male might perform the sky dance at two or more locations, he will dance at one site more than the others.

If you want to attend a sky dance, you need to arrive early, before the sun sets. The best seats are on the eastern side of the stage. Looking toward the western horizon, the light provided by the setting sun will permit you to watch the performance longer into the night.

Settle in at a concealed location that provides a good view of the performance. Make yourself comfortable and wait. As the light of day fades and finally reaches an intensity of only 0.05-foot candles, Mother Nature, the director of the show, sends a male woodcock onto the stage.

The star of the show flies in and lands on the ground. Often, a female and other males will arrive about the same time the dominant male makes his appearance. These additional males are the equivalent of onstage extras and don't involve themselves in the courtship activities.

When we attend a theatrical performance, the actors are performing for the entertainment of the audience. Here, far from bright theater lights, the actor is focused on trying to please only one member of the audience—the female.

The curtain rises, revealing the male standing in the singing ground with its bill resting on its chest. Silence permeates the early night air. Without warning, a loud *peent* is heard. This is the first of what will become a series of *peents* uttered by the male every two to four seconds for the next minute or so.

Then, again without warning, the male leaps into the air, flying skyward in spirals that become tighter the higher the bird flies. As the woodcock makes its ascent, it produces a pleasant twittering sound that becomes louder even as the bird seems to be disappearing from sight some two hundred to three hundred feet above the woodland amphitheater. Just when the bird reaches the apex of its flight, the twittering is replaced with a soft, musical warble, and the bird tumbles downward. Just before it crashes into the ground, the bird catches its fall and lands softly on the singing ground, often in the same spot from where it took flight. The whole aerial display lasts anywhere from forty to fifty seconds.

These dramatic performances last for about an hour, during which time the male makes nine to thirteen flights. The whole show is then reenacted at dawn. However, under a full moon, the sky dance will continue as long as the moon bathes the landscape in its pallid light. The sky dance isn't performed, though, when temperatures dip below freezing.

This engagement lasts for several weeks, with females joining males on the singing grounds until they begin nesting. In Monroe County, nesting can begin as early as February. In fact, one February, I found a woodcock nest surrounded by patches of snow.

Patrons of the theater will tell you that a good gauge of the quality of a play is how long it runs on Broadway. The longest-running plays like *The Phantom of the Opera, Cats,* or *Les Misérables* are performed thousands of times during runs that can span a couple of decades or so. The sky dance of the American woodcock has been acted out millions of times during a run that has lasted for thousands of years. Obviously, if you enjoy nature and good entertainment, this is one show you can't afford to miss.

January 16, 2002

THE PLIGHT OF THE WOODCOCK

The American woodcock has a special place in my heart. When I began hunting as a teenager many years ago, the first bird I bagged was a woodcock. Since that time, I have hunted, watched, and researched this fascinating game bird from the Canadian border to Alabama and Georgia. Consequently, when I learned that this year's woodcock season is only twenty-nine days long, stretching from December 22 through January 20—during which time a hunter can bag only three woodcocks per day—my heart was heavy.

In the not-too-distant past, the woodcock was one of the most popular game birds in North America. As late as 1990, some two million woodcocks were bagged. However, for more than three decades, woodcock populations have been steadily declining. During this time frame, woodcock populations in the eastern United States and Canada have plummeted 2.5 percent annually. Clearly, if the woodcock population continues to decline at such a rapid pace, the specter of further reductions in the length of the woodcock hunting season and bag limit looms on the horizon.

The woodcock is one of our most interesting game birds. Although it is considered a sandpiper, don't look for it along the white sands of coastal Georgia. The American woodcock prefers young hardwood forests, brushy areas, old fields, and forest openings along rivers and stream courses.

The woodcock is slightly larger than a bobwhite. Its plumage is mottled brown, and black bars run across its head. Its long bill (two and a half inches) is flexible and equipped with nerves that detect even the slightest movement of its favorite food, the earthworm.

The woodcock is a migratory game bird. While the woodcock breeds as far south as Georgia and Florida, its principal breeding range is centered in central to eastern Canada and the northeastern United States. The bird winters throughout the Southeast, although wintering populations are highest in Louisiana.

In spite of the fact that wildlife biologists have been studying the woodcock for years, they have yet to pinpoint the cause of the bird's alarming decline. Currently, researchers are looking at habitat changes and loss on both the breeding and wintering grounds, hunting, and environmental pollution as the most probable suspects responsible for dwindling woodcock numbers.

Many researchers believe that habitat loss is at the top of this short list of potential culprits; however, more research needs to be done before the blame can be firmly attributed to it.

What we do know is that the landscape of the northeastern United States and Canada changed dramatically during the past century. During this time, the forested areas that had been devastated during the nineteenth century matured and became less desirable to the woodcock. In addition, the thousands of small farms that were the cornerstones of the economy in this part of the world during the early part of the twentieth century steadily disappeared. These farmsteads provided ideal habitats for the woodcock. They contained young forests, small fields, and wetlands as well as forest clearings—all prime woodcock habitats. As farmers left the land for jobs in cities and towns, the farms quickly reverted to forests and lost their value to the woodcock as roosting, feeding, breeding, and brood-rearing sites.

While this was going on, the face of the rural south was also being transformed. Small farms were disappearing here too. In addition, thousands of acres of prime woodcock habitat were converted to large agricultural fields, subdivisions, parking lots, shopping malls, and pine plantations. Indeed, the woodcock was dealt a double whammy.

The role of environmental contaminants is less obvious. We do know that earthworms make up more than 80 percent of the woodcock's diet. We also know that earthworms are very sensitive to environmental pollutants.

In 1996, Canadian wildlife biologists made a startling discovery. They found that woodcock contained extremely high concentrations of lead, particularly in Quebec and the Maritime provinces. In fact, the woodcock tested harbored two to three times more lead than ducks. The researchers are unsure how the birds became so contaminated. The birds don't ingest lead shot like ducks. Perhaps they obtained the lead from the earthworms they eat. They are also trying to determine whether or not the lead came from spent lead shot slowly decomposing in the soil, pesticides, pollution from factories, or perhaps even leaded gas. In addition, biologists want to know what impact, if any, the lead pollution is having on woodcock reproduction.

Before wildlife biologists can begin to reverse the woodcock's downward population trend, they must identify the cause of the declines. Hopefully, the culprit(s) will soon be revealed—before it is too late. It would be a shame if future generations of hunters were denied the thrill of flushing a woodcock from an alder thicket on a crisp fall morning.

HOW DO I DEAL WITH AN ANGRY BIRD?

For weeks, a friend of mine has been telling me that a bird has been waking him up, incessantly tapping on his bedroom window. Not being an early riser, he is concerned that this irritation doesn't seem to show any promise of ending soon.

In the not-too-distant past, when superstition reigned supreme, the bird's strange behavior would not be considered a minor annoyance. Indeed, anyone experiencing such a problem would be gripped by fear. This is because they believed that window-tapping birds were actually the souls of the dead trying to find a way to enter a home and lead someone residing there away from the world of the living into the afterlife.

Today we know that the real reason for the odd behavior is far less blood chilling. Birds that tap or otherwise attack windows and other reflective surfaces are actually trying to defend their breeding territory. When a bird sees its reflection, it believes it is actually face-to-face with a rival bent on taking over an area in which it hopes to woo a mate. That being the case, the interloper has got to go. Thus, the bird vigorously attacks its imagined foe. Regardless of how energetically and long it attacks the bird, though, it never leaves, and thus, day after day, it returns to valiantly fight again. Although these defenders are literally fearless, they rarely cause injury to themselves or the reflective surface they are attacking. However, as any who have dealt with the problem can attest, for some reason they will often leave a mess behind. Perhaps they are trying to add the ultimate insult to injury.

Birds that fight their reflections have strong territorial instincts and are members of species that are most likely to nest near our homes. My friend's bird is a male eastern towhee. Among the other birds that engage in this bizarre activity are cardinals, mockingbirds, bluebirds, and even summer tanagers. I also know of a church located in Stone Mountain where the parishioners have seen an American crow as well a turkey gobbler attack their reflections in the church's large windows for days on end.

Although these birds most often fight windows, their next favorite target seems to be car mirrors. However, they will also assault other reflective objects, such as hubcaps and shiny pots.

One woman told me that a male cardinal was attacking her shiny red sports car. She asked me if the cardinal thought her car was a giant cardinal. I told her that I didn't know, but if he did, his epic struggle would be the bird world's version of the biblical tale of David and Goliath.

Several years ago when the G8 Summit was held on Georgia's Sea Island, another cardinal decided this was the time to attack the windows of the meeting room where many of the free world's most powerful leaders were gathered to discuss the world's worsening economic condition. I'm sure that to the bird, the world's economic woes were not nearly as important as its need to keep another male cardinal away from its turf.

A woman who lives in the south Georgia town of Chauncey recently called to tell me that when two bluebirds recently began attacking one of her windows, she thought they were cute. However, since these skirmishes had gone on for weeks, and the battlefield expanded to include the mirrors of any cars parked in her yard as well as the windows on all sides of her house, she was ready for the pugnacious birds to find something better to do with their time and energy.

Such problems beg the question, "How do I deal with an angry bird?"

As you might expect, there is no simple answer. What works for one person may not work for another. However, all of the solutions that have worked in the past involve preventing the birds from seeing their reflections.

If a bird is attacking car or truck mirrors, cover the mirrors with plastic grocery bags. If you try this, don't forget to remove the bags before you jump into your vehicle and head to town.

When the altercations are directed at a window, you might consider placing a screen over it. Or you can tack a piece of crop netting over the window some two to three inches away from the windowpane. Use netting with holes small enough to prevent the birds from becoming entangled in it. Also, stretch the netting tight enough so that if a bird strikes the netting, it will harmlessly bounce off.

Some people have solved their problem by mounting wooden grills over their windows. Others have met with success by applying closely spaced strips of colored tape over the window glass. I have even heard of homeowners rubbing soap on their windows in an effort to dull the surface of the window enough to prevent reflections.

One of the newer devices that can help solve this perplexing problem is one-way transparent film. The film comes in a variety of designs that can be easily applied and removed.

If your patience with one of these bird Casanovas is quickly running out, don't despair—as the breeding season begins to wane, it will soon turn its attention to more mundane matters.

PART 2

Reptiles and Amphibians

FOWLER'S TOADS ARE FASCINATING

We all have our favorites. We have favorite baseball and football teams. Everyone has favorite foods. We also cherish favorite songs, performers, movies—you name it. Indeed, a list of our personal favorites goes on and on. Well, I have a favorite that probably won't turn up on your list. I have a favorite toad. Let me explain how I came to have a favorite toad.

My favorite toad is Fowler's toad. It is named for a nineteenth-century Massachusetts naturalist named S. P. Fowler. Fowler described the species some 155 years ago.

When my granddaughter was a few years younger, she loved to capture toads. From spring into summer, we spent many enjoyable hours roaming around the house under the cloak of darkness, scanning the ground with our flashlights and looking for toads. When we spotted one, she would try to grab it before it disappeared under the shrubbery. She quickly became quite proficient in the art of toad catching. As a result, she would often catch a half dozen or more in a single evening.

I can't begin to tell you how much fun we both had on our nocturnal adventures. It provided a great opportunity to spend some quality time with her. Additionally, using the yard as an outdoor classroom, both of us learned a lot about one of the animals that lives just outside our back door.

The toads she caught were Fowler's toads, the toads we are most likely to find here in the county. It is some two to three inches long and has a light stripe that runs down the length of its back. As is the case with all toads, it has a warty skin. The toad's skin color can vary anywhere from brown or gray to brick red. The toads we found were typically red. Fowler's toad also usually has six dark-brown or black spots on its back. If you closely examine these distinctive spots, you will note that each contains three or more tiny warts. Also, the large glands (parotid) located behind its eyes actually touch a distinctive ridge (postorbital) that runs around the back and inside of the toad's eyes.

Although four toads are found in Georgia, the only other true toad you are likely to find locally is the American toad. However, in most cases, you will find more Fowler's toads than American toads.

The American toad is slightly larger than Fowler's toad. The glands located behind its eyes do not touch the ridge at the back of its eye. It too usually possesses a light-colored band that runs down its back. In addition, if you closely examine the dark spots on the toad's back, you will discover that each contains only one or two tiny warts. The color of its warty skin ranges all the way from dark red to gray and brown.

I must confess that I am a novice toad watcher. However, some veteran toad watchers swear they can tell a Fowler's from an American toad while speeding down the highway. They claim that American toads try to escape oncoming traffic by taking long hops. Fowler's toads, on the other hand, make far shorter hops. Hmm…that is something I will have to see to believe!

You are apt to find Fowler's toads in a variety of locations. They live in agricultural areas as well and in both moist and dry woodlands. Most of us become acquainted with them around our homes. In fact, they are probably the most common amphibian living in our yards.

We sometimes stumble across them during the day; however, unless it is cloudy and humid, they prefer to spend their days in burrows or beneath rocks or other objects. Typically, they are most active at sunset and during the night.

Unless it is their mating season, when they are out and about, they are hunting for insects and a host of other invertebrates that make up their diet. A favorite feeding spot is beneath outside lights.

Like all toads, this nocturnal animal must return to water to breed. Since no open water is located close to my home, I would dearly love to know just how far the adult Fowler's toads living in my yard go to breed.

The toad's breeding season runs from April to August. During this important time of the year, males and females head toward open water. These breeding sites may be as small as temporary pools and farm ponds to the shallow edges of reservoirs.

Once the males arrive, they form large groups named choruses and begin to call in an attempt to attract mates. The call is described as a one- to four-second nasal bleat that sounds like *w-a-a-a-h*. While the call is not very pleasing to our ears, to a female Fowler's toad, it is a love song.

After mating, the female lays anywhere from seven thousand to ten thousand eggs in long, coiled, gelatinous, double strands. The eggs hatch within a week. During the next forty to sixty days, the tadpoles that emerged from the eggs transform into tiny replicas of their parents and leave their watery home to spend their lives on dry land.

With the arrival of cold weather in the fall, Fowler's toads retreat to burrows, where they hibernate until spring.

The other night, as I was walking to my home office, I spotted a toad hopping down the path my granddaughter and I walked so many times on our toad hunts a few years ago. I couldn't help but stop briefly and recall how Fowler's toads helped nurture the love between a little girl and her granddad and helped forge a bond between her and the natural world.

That is why I have a favorite toad.

WATER MOCCASIN OR WATERSNAKE—
THAT IS THE QUESTION

Recently, while golfing at a course in Lamar County, I went looking for a wayward shot skillfully plunked into a water hazard and found a banded watersnake that had been recently killed. I told my playing partner that I was sure a golfer had killed the poor snake believing he had dispatched a dreaded water moccasin (also known as the cottonmouth).

A few holes later, when we drove up to a tee where a golfer was waiting to hit his tee shot, the first thing out of the golfer's mouth was, "The two guys ahead of us said they killed a water moccasin a couple of holes back. Did you see it?" The young golfer was surprised when I told him that we found the snake and that it wasn't a water moccasin and had posed no threat to the golfers.

I don't know what it is about snakes that are found near water. It seems that most people assume they must be cottonmouths. Actually, in this neck of the woods, while water moccasins are sometimes found here, they are rare. I have waded through Monroe

County beaver ponds for more than thirty-five years and never encountered a cottonmouth. More than likely, a snake found near water in Monroe County is a harmless watersnake.

The ranges of three watersnakes—the plain-bellied, northern (also known as the midland), and brown—blanket Monroe County. The northern is the most common watersnake found in the county. In comparison, the cottonmouth is typically found only in extreme south Monroe County.

However, because these nonpoisonous water snakes are so often mistaken for water moccasins, they are routinely shot, hacked, or beaten to death by people that are deathly afraid that they pose a threat. This is unfortunate, as these snakes aren't dangerous.

Here are a few tips that can help you tell the difference between a cottonmouth and a watersnake.

Although watersnakes and cottonmouths live near water, watersnakes are usually found along streams and large ponds and reservoirs. Meanwhile, cottonmouths prefer to live along slow-moving creeks and rivers.

If you take a close look at a northern watersnake's bands, you will note that they are broader on top than the sides. While some large adult cottonmouths are dark and show no pattern, most display bands that are widest on the sides. This gives each band an hourglass appearance.

Contrary to popular belief, you can't tell a cottonmouth from a watersnake by the shapes of their heads. Although the cottonmouth has a triangular-shaped head, when the watersnake is agitated, it will flatten its head, thereby giving it a triangular appearance.

The water moccasin has a small pit in front of each eye. It also has elliptical pupils. Water snakes don't have the pits, and their pupils are round.

You might be surprised to learn that the inner linings of the mouths of both snakes are white. When startled, the cottonmouth will hold its head at an angle and open its mouth, displaying its white interior.

Another difference can be found on the underside these snakes' tails. The scales located on the underside of a cottonmouth are arranged in a single row. In comparison, the scales on the underside of a watersnake's tail are grouped into two rows.

Finally, watersnakes typically swim low in the water and will often dive below the surface when harassed, cottonmouths swim with most of their bodies above the surface of the water. They will also often hold their heads above the water.

In truth, the cottonmouth doesn't deserve its bad reputation. These large snakes will not attack you on sight. In fact, they are retiring creatures that would rather avoid a confrontation. Even when this poisonous snake is harassed, it will often not strike. Instead, it gapes its mouth to show its white interior as a warning, not as an act of aggression.

While cottonmouth bites are rare, those that do occur are often the result of somebody trying to kill, capture, or harass the snake. Consequently, if you see a cottonmouth, the safest thing to do is not disturb it. Simply walk away, and leave the snake alone.

February 6, 2002

THIS FROG IS A FALSE PROPHET

For the past few weeks, we have been enjoying unseasonably warm weather. Many flowering plants have responded to this rare winter respite. Forsythia, narcissus, flowering quince, and other plants have burst into bloom long before Mother Nature had planned for them to stage their floral show. If you have spent any time outside on these warm winter nights, you have probably heard the incessant calling of frogs. The calls, which sound much like a fingernail being dragged across the teeth of a comb, are made by the upland chorus frog.

For those looking for any sign that winter is over, the *creek* call of the chorus frog is a harbinger of spring. In truth, the chorus frog is a false prophet. Chorus frogs are winter breeders. Whenever temperatures warm during the winter, male chorus frogs are apt to begin calling in hopes of attracting a mate. Typically, when spring finally arrives, calling and breeding are already on the wane.

The chorus frog breeding season commences as early as November and runs as late as March. Should the fickle winter weather take a turn for the worse, the chorus frog can be frozen solid only to hop away unscathed when the ice thaws.

Few animals share this remarkable ability. Typically, when ice crystals form in an animal's body, they destroy tissues. The chorus frog survives because the ice gathers in places away from its vital organs, such as the heart and lungs. The ice within a frozen chorus frog is situated in the stomach and bladder as well as beneath the skin.

Should you encounter a frozen chorus frog, it would be next to impossible to determine whether or not the amphibian is alive or dead. The animal would have only the faintest nerve activity. Its heart and breathing would have stopped.

While most Monroe Countians have heard the chorus frog, few of us have actually seen one. It is a small frog, measuring only three-quarters of an inch to one and a half inches in length. A distinctive pale line runs along its upper lip. It also displays a dark spot between its eyes and three stripes down its back. A dark stripe runs through the eye down the side to the thigh. The body is brown or gray.

Male chorus frogs usually call at night. However, they will also get cranked up on cloudy days. The frogs call from small patches of water in woodlands, grassy areas, wooded swamps, and forests adjoining streams and ponds.

You are most likely to find a chorus frog when it is calling; however, even then, you need a lot of luck to spot one. When the frog senses something approaching, it quickly dives underwater.

Outside the breeding season, they are rarely seen, preferring to spend most of their time beneath the ground. At times, farmers uncover them as they plow fields.

Female chorus frogs lay upward of one thousand eggs during a breeding season. These eggs are laid in batches of sixty or so. Egg clusters are attached to aquatic vegetation.

Depending on the temperature of the water, it takes two to three months for the eggs to hatch and the tadpoles to mature into frogs that can leave their watery home.

If you are looking for a great way to unwind at the end of the day, sit outside in your lawn chair, and listen to the sounds of the night. If it is a warm evening, chances are that you will hear the calling of hundreds of chorus frogs. Their chorus has been heard for thousands of winters. Native Americans listened to them long before the first Europeans reached Monroe County. It was heard during two world wars. Let's hope it will never be muted—it reminds us that we are never apart from the natural world.

PART 3

Insects and Such

FRAGILE TREASURES

As far as backyards go, mine is far from the largest, best trimmed, or, in the eyes of many, the most beautiful. However, I would not trade it for any other.

In spite of its unassuming appearance, it is a place where treasure has been found. Although I am not talking about jewels or gold coins, the discoveries made in my yard are still priceless. They make up a treasure trove of family experiences with the plants and animals that live just outside the back door. My wife and I have never used a treasure map to guide my daughter and granddaughter on backyard journeys of exploration. In fact, more often than not, all of our best finds are made serendipitously.

When the girls were younger, we were their guides, teaching them to use their senses of sight, hearing, smell, and touch when outdoors. However, it didn't take them long to begin venturing out and making their own finds. Now, the distinction between the guide and the guided is often blurred.

For example, a few weeks ago, our eight-year old granddaughter happened to notice the light-brownish nymphal skin shed by a recently emerged adult cicada (often called a locust) attached to a pillar beneath my home office. Immediately, she wanted to know what it was. This provided me the opportunity to tell her about these insects, whose buzzing mating calls are one of the sounds of summer.

My wife went on to suggest that she might find others if she looked around the yard. Soon, I noticed her looking for other shed skins on the trunks of trees. In a short time, she had dozens of the fragile casings. Later that evening, my wife found that she had neatly lined up her discoveries on a shelf in her bedroom. What might have been overlooked and considered valueless by most are undoubtedly treasures to her.

The cicada is just the most recent in a long list of animals the girls have encountered on backyard forays.

Years ago, my wife introduced our daughter to the ant lion, or doodle bug. She pointed out to her how these strange little creatures excavate sandy funnels and wait at the bottom for a hapless ant or other small insect to venture into its deadly trap. She went on to demonstrate how you can coax the doodle bug from its hiding place by gently stroking the sides of the funnel with a blade of grass while repeating, "Doodle bug, doodle bug, come out—your house is on fire."

I will never forget teaching my granddaughter how to use a spincasting rod. I tied a rubber worm to the line and let her practice casting. As she slowly reeled in the artificial worm after a long cast, an American robin, apparently mistaking the lure for the real thing, flew down and chased it back toward us. The expression on my granddaughter's face as she watched the bird's antics are forever etched in my memory.

Over the years, the girls have helped me build and paint countless nest boxes. They are excited when one is used by bluebirds, nuthatches, or chickadees and always enjoy peeking inside the boxes for quick glimpses of fragile eggs and fuzzy nestlings.

They enjoy helping me restock our bird feeders and watch a veritable parade of birds that dine at my wildlife smorgasbord. And they seem to take delight in watching my often futile attempts to thwart gray squirrels from eating more than their share of my seed offering.

The wild and cultivated plants growing in our yard have always fascinated the girls. They enjoy looking for the first crocus poking out of the ground in the spring, admiring the beauty of a dogwood blossom, sucking nectar from a honeysuckle bloom, and collecting fall leaves seemingly dipped in a kaleidoscope of colors.

The girls have also discovered that birds, deer, and other critters enjoy eating the apples, pears, blueberries, and figs that ripen in our yard as much as we do. One summer day, my wife and granddaughter were surprised to find that we were sharing figs with a hummingbird. As they peered out the bedroom window, a hummingbird flew down and dipped its bill into the sweet fig juice welling up in a hole punched into a fig by a summer tanager.

Our outdoor adventures don't stop when the sun goes down. Even on cold winter nights, we venture out to view the constellations, comets, and falling stars.

In the spring, we sit outside, listening for the calls of whip-poor-wills and chuck-will's widows.

In summer, we all enjoy watching fireflies blinking as they slowly navigate across the yard.

My granddaughter enjoys catching toads at night. Once caught, each toad is closely examined and released to continue its nocturnal search for insects.

For the past two years, my daughter and granddaughter have joined me in trying to attract moths and other nighttime insects with a sheet illuminated by a black light. I am sure that my neighbors and people driving past my yard wonder what in the world we are doing as we move about in the darkness around an eerie blue light. Through the magic of the black light, we have discovered scores of beautiful moths and some of the strangest-looking bee-tles, leafhoppers, and other insects that I have ever seen.

Space has allowed me to share only a smattering of priceless treasures my family has found in our backyard. I urge you to begin embarking on backyard forays with your children and grandchil-dren. You will be amazed how the discovery of something as small as a lady bug can stimulate their curiosity. Seeing their expressions as they find a backyard treasure is something you will never forget. You will soon realize that you are having as much fun as they are and that you are giving them the invaluable gift of heightening their sense of wonder and appreciation for those plants and ani-mals with which they share the world.

LUNA MOTHS—NIGHTTIME BEAUTIES

One of my favorite insects is the luna moth. Locally, we can see it from March through September; however, I have yet to spot one this year. I attribute this to our unusual spring weather. As we all know, the appearances of a number of plants and animals seem behind schedule this year. Now that the cold, wet weather seems to be behind us, I am anxiously awaiting my first encounter with a moth that many believe is our most beautiful insect.

If you have never cast your eyes on a luna moth, you are in for a real treat. As far as moths go, it is large. From wing tip to wing tip, it can measure more than four inches. Its translucent wings are lime green and etched with thin, yellowish-white veins. Adorning each of its front wings is a small, clear, moon-shaped eyespot. In fact, these eyespots are responsible for its name. The moth is named after Luna, the Roman goddess of the moon. The leading edge of the wings can vary from reddish brown and purple and pink in individuals that we see at this time of year to yellow in those that emerge in summer. The hind wings are long, ribbon-like, and slightly curled. The insect's stout body is covered with fine white hairs. The moth's antennae are featherlike. As is the case with other moths, the male's antennae are larger than those sported by females. To top it all off, the luna moth's legs are dark pink.

Since luna moths are nocturnal, I rarely get to see one on the wing. However, when I do spot one in the air, it reminds me of a woodland fairy princess bedecked in a stunning green gown dancing in the night sky.

In truth, adult luna moths are in a race against the clock. From the time they emerge from their cocoons, they live only a week or so. During this all-too-brief period, they never eat or drink. They live strictly on food they stored in their bodies as fat when they were caterpillars.

Typically, luna moths leave their cocoons in midmorning. As soon as they emerge, they climb to a perch and begin pumping fluid into their wings. By nightfall, the wings are inflated, and the moths are ready to take wing. Obviously, males and females must find one another before mating can take place. Females aid the process by emitting a scent that is detected by the males' large antennae. Mating usually takes place after midnight.

Upon mating, the females immediately begin laying eggs on the leaves of specific plants. These plants are called host plants. These plants will provide food for the caterpillars that hatch from the tiny eggs. My mentor on moth biology tells me that in these parts, the host plants most often used by lunas are sweetgum, followed by persimmon, wild cherry, sumac, and hickory. Eggs are usually laid four to seven at a time. A female luna moth will lay some one hundred to three hundred eggs in her lifetime.

The tiny caterpillars hatch in only seven to twelve days and don't waste any time before gorging themselves on the leaves of its host plant. During the four to six weeks the moths spend as caterpillars, they will increase their weight by more than four thousand times! In fact, these eating machines grow and grow until they are ready to outgrow their skin. Then, they go through a molt that leaves them with a completely new skin. This happens four times before they reach some three inches in length.

After the final molt, the caterpillar falls or crawls to the ground and spins its paper-thin cocoon. Here it will remain while the remarkable process of metamorphosis takes place. This process can take as little as two to three weeks during the spring and summer. However, it can take several months for those that overwinter.

Should you happen to find a luna cocoon, if you hold it up to the light, you can often see a live pupa inside.

While encased in the cocoon, the caterpillar almost magically transforms from a green, grub-like creature into the stunningly beautiful adult luna moth. This remarkable process is one of the most amazing transformations in nature.

When the moth is ready to leave its cocoon, it will move about, trying to break free of its silky prison.

Outside lighting poses one of the greatest threats to these magnificent moths. Male lunas are drawn to mercury-vapor lights, which are often used to illuminate parking lots and highways. This can hinder the males' efforts to find mates during their all too brief lifespan. Females, on the other hand, will also come to lights after they have laid their eggs. Consequently, as rural areas have become more developed, the impact of these lights has increased dramatically in the past several decades. Where this has occurred, it has been reported that luna moth populations have decreased. Fortunately, mercury-vapor lights are increasingly being replaced by sodium lights that are less expensive to purchase and operate.

If you happen to spot a luna moth hanging motionless on a tree or building, don't disturb it. It is awaiting the return of darkness, when it will once again take to the air to ensure it leaves behind another generation of one of Mother Nature's most beautiful treasures.

October 21, 2009

BIG YELLOW BUTTERFLIES

For the past few weeks, it has been next to impossible to go outside and not see a plethora of big, bright, lemon-yellow butterflies. If you have wondered what they are and why we are seeing so many right now, read on.

These butterflies are named cloudless sulphurs. They sport wingspans measuring roughly two and a quarter to three inches in width.

Males and females look pretty much alike. However, if you take a close look at them as they feed at zinnias or other flowers growing in your yard, you will see that all are adorned with two silvery spots near the middle of their closed hindwings. Some of these butterflies will display a few small, scattered reddish marks while others are marked with large reddish blotches. If you really want to impress your friends, you can tell them that the males are the ones with just a few marks on the undersides of their wings while the females are those with the larger markings.

Earlier in the year, I was beginning to wonder what happened to the cloudless sulphurs. I wasn't seeing many in my backyard, and few were seen during the annual Fourth of July Butterfly Count. These fears proved to be premature. Lately, I have seen as many as if not more cloudless sulphurs than I have in past years.

One reason we have been seeing so many cloudless sulphurs in the county is that we are witnessing this butterfly's fall migration. I know what you are saying: "I thought monarchs were the only butterflies that migrated." Such is not the case. A number of our familiar butterflies, including common buckeyes, red admirals, American ladies, and long-tailed skippers, migrate too.

The cloudless sulphur migration begins in late summer. Using the sun as their compass, cloudless sulphurs from as far away as Canada begin winging their way south. Remarkably, these fragile insects are able to migrate about twelve miles a day as they make their way into Florida and beyond.

Males reach the wintering grounds first, rarely stopping long enough to feed. Meanwhile, females travel southward at a more leisurely pace, stopping often to dine heavily before moving on. I suspect that because these butterflies are so intent on refueling before resuming their trek, at this time of year you can more easily approach cloudless sulphurs than at any other time of the year.

Many biologists theorize that the females' slower-paced migration allows them to reach their wintering grounds with more energy reserves, thereby enhancing their ability to lay eggs.

While the cloudless sulphur's migration is little known by most folks nowadays, chances are it was observed by such notables as Christopher Columbus and Charles Darwin. Entries in the journals of both describe clouds of sulphurs seen on their voyages through the Caribbean. Although I personally have not seen cloudless sulphurs flying out over the ocean, I have found thousands washed ashore on the beaches of Sapelo Island on the Georgia coast.

At the same time, cloudless sulphurs are heading south, some are actually flying north. Biologists don't have an explanation for this bizarre behavior. One thing is certain, though—those hapless butterflies that migrate north will soon succumb to winter's frigid temperatures.

Cloudless sulphurs overwinter as adults. Although they are more cold hardy than many butterflies, only a few try to overwinter in Monroe County. Those that do winter here spend the majority of their time in sheltered areas. As such, they can be seen locally throughout the winter, flying about on warm days.

Once spring bursts forth, cloudless sulphurs begin migrating north. Interestingly, the northward migration is but a shadow of the spectacular fall migration.

As the butterflies wing north, they lay eggs on partridge pea and other closely related plants. When a new generation of cloudless sulphurs emerges and develops into adults, many of these butterflies head northward. Consequently, by the end of the summer, the butterflies are prospering all the way to Canada. The pace of the spring migration is greatly affected by weather. This helps explain why cloudless sulphurs were so scarce earlier this year and are so common now.

If you want to attract cloudless sulphurs to your yard at this time of the year, I would recommend that you add Turk's cap and pine-apple sage to your landscape. Both have bright red blooms and act like cloudless-sulphur magnets. Other late-blooming plants that are great sources of nectar for resident and migrating butterflies in your yard include goldenrod, aster, swamp sunflower, liatris (blazing star), zinnia, salvia, and Georgia mint.

Enjoy this annual fall spectacle while you can. Shortly, it will be over, and the cold weather will be upon us.

July 25, 2010

ROBBER FLIES—SCARY PREDATORS

The robber fly isn't the largest or smallest insect in your yard. It isn't even the most striking. In fact, when you take a close look at one, you will find that it is scary enough to star in a horror movie. Perhaps its only claim to fame is that it is one of the most ferocious predators you will ever see.

While I am sure you have seen this top predator, you may not have given it even a second glance, let alone recognize it as a formidable predator. The nine hundred some odd species that inhabit North America vary widely in size. Some are only half an inch long. At the other end of the spectrum, others reach two inches in length. Most are drab and look much like large, long-legged house flies. Many have quite slender hairy abdomens with hunched backs. However, it is their heads that grab your attention. Their large eyes face sideways instead of straight ahead. Additionally, the tops of their heads sharply dip between their eyes.

And then there is its beak. This lethal weapon is stiff and festooned with bristly hairs. Hiding within the beak is an extremely sharp, knifelike structure.

Robber flies hunt from perches. Such perches can be a twig, leaf, or other object that offers an excellent view of the fly's surroundings. Robber flies often use the same perch day after day.

One summer, a fairly large robber fly selected a bare twig on a tree outside my office window as its perch. Each day I watched this flying predator fly off its perch, trying to capture prey in midair. After each foray, it would return to the same spot and wait for the next potential victim to pass by.

If you observe a robber fly for any length of time, it quickly becomes apparent that this predator eats a wide variety of critters, including many that are much larger than the robber fly itself. Among the vast array of insects eaten by robber flies are butterflies and moths, beetles, grasshoppers, flies, and bees. Being a true cannibal, they will also eat other robber flies. In fact, female robber flies have been known to devour potential mates.

Throughout the day, robber flies are constantly in an attack mode. When one spots a hapless insect venturing too close to its perch, it immediately takes wing and tries to chase it down. If the hunter is successful, it will grab the beast around the head and back and clamp down. It then thrusts its daggerlike beak deep into the insect's thorax or head. The hairs surrounding the fly's beak help hold the knifelike beak in the wound while it injects a lethal concoction of digestive juices and nerve toxins. The deadly brew renders the prey helpless and quickly liquefies its body tissues.

After it has subdued its prey, the robber fly lands and slurps up the nutrient-rich insides of the insect. Once its meal is complete, the robber fly simply drops the empty exoskeleton of its prey and returns to its hunting perch to await its next victim.

Since the robber fly is a creature of habit, if you patiently watch one hunt, you can locate the spot where the predator dines. There you will find the numerous discarded hulls of its victims.

Fortunately, robber flies don't pose a threat to us. In fact, about the only time they will bite us is when we try to handle them.

The robber fly is often called the bee killer. It is so named because, much to the chagrin of beekeepers, it will sometimes set up its hunting territory close to beehives. From a nearby perch, the aerial killer will dine throughout the day on the constant stream of workers that fly in and out of a hive.

However, when a robber fly, also dubbed the assassin fly, patrols our gardens and dines on a wide array of garden pests, we consider it a valuable insect.

Regardless of whether you consider the robber fly a pest or a valued neighbor, it remains one of the most scary looking and fascinating critters that inhabits our yards.

July 24, 2002

CICADA KILLERS ARE PATROLLING YOUR BACKYARD

Our biggest native wasp goes by the daunting name of cicada killer. This mammoth of the wasp world can reach two or more inches in length. While its large size and striking black-and-yellow markings make it easy to spot, most folks have never seen this backyard resident. When one is spotted, it is often mistaken for a yellow jacket on steroids. Although its size is impressive, the insect's life history is even more remarkable.

Cicada killers make their first appearance in early summer (late June and early July), when they emerge from special chambers their mothers constructed the previous summer. It is no coincidence that their emergence coincides with the appearance of cicadas. They are most often seen on golf courses, lawns, and athletic fields. Reason would suggest that you would look upward to spot a wasp. Such is not the case with the cicada killer. You are most likely to see one by looking down. Keep your eyes peeled for a giant wasp digging a burrow or visiting your flower gardens.

Sometimes you can even find them feeding on food left behind after a picnic.

The cicada killer is aptly named. This solitary wasp preys upon cicadas. Cicadas are those large insects that make that strange, monotonous buzzing sound on hot summer days.

Male cicada killers appear about two weeks ahead of the females. Almost immediately, the males set about staking out territories. These areas are rarely more than sixty-five feet from where they hatch. Interestingly, males can be taken and moved up to a mile away, and they will return unerringly to the place where they were captured.

The male's sole purpose for living is to mate. Consequently, during his short two-week life as an adult, he spends most of his time defending his territory from other males and watching for a female.

As for the females, as soon as they see the light of day, the males try to mate with them. Some research suggests that the females attract prospective suitors by emitting an odor (pheromone). The females mate but once in spite of the fact that many males often vie for the privilege.

Once the adult females mate, they spend the first two weeks of their brief twenty-four- to twenty-eight-day adult life span reconnoitering the landscape in search of suitable places to dig the burrows in which they will lay their eggs. While they are able to dig in our hard, red, clay soil, they prefer sandy loam. Typically, cicada killers choose open sites that face the southeast and are adjacent to hardwood trees. Since ideal nesting sites are sometimes hard to find, the same areas are used annually by the large wasps.

As soon as a suitable area is located, females excavate burrows that can range from ten inches to three feet long and some two feet below the surface of the ground. At the end of the burrow, the female fashions several spherical nest chambers. The entrance to a burrow is large enough for you to slip your finger into. Although the cicada killer is considered a solitary nester, often many cicada killers will dig nesting burrows in close proximity to one another. After the nesting chambers have been completed, everything is ready for the next step in this insect's fascinating life history.

The female must now capture a cicada. She does this by sitting on a perch and waiting for the appearance of her hapless prey. It was once thought that females caught only males that she located by the familiar buzzing sound made only by the male cicadas. Most entomologists now agree that the cicada killer locates its prey by sight and sound, as they catch both male and female cicadas.

Most of the cicadas are captured in midair. Once she has latched onto a cicada, she injects it with venom. This venom paralyzes the cicada in about a minute. She then flies to her burrow, carrying the cicada in an upside-down position. Although the female cicada killer is twice as large as the male, she still has trouble carrying prey, which often weighs twice as much as she does. Often, a cicada killer will climb up the trunk of a tree with her prey so that she can launch herself into the air from a higher elevation. At times, even this doesn't help. Consequently, females are sometimes seen carrying their prey across the ground en route to their burrows. In some instances, a cicada killer will drop her prey and not retrieve it. This often explains why we find apparently healthy cicadas on the ground, unable to fly.

Once she reaches her burrow, the cicada killer places one to three paralyzed cicadas in each chamber. These paralyzed insects will actually live about twice as long as those that aren't caught and injected with venom by a cicada killer. In exchange for their extended lives, they will serve as food for the young cicada killers. Indeed, the developing larva literally eats the cicada alive!

After the cicada killer lays her eggs, she will close the entrance to the hole and even camouflage it.

The eggs are laid under the second leg of the cicada. It is thought that this is the best position for the young cicada killer to begin devouring the cicada.

Researchers have discovered that the female cicada killer actually determines the sex of her offspring. It seems that male cicadas are only produced from unfertilized eggs. By the same token, females are produced only from fertilized eggs.

If a female places only one cicada in a chamber, the egg placed on the cicada will invariably hatch into a male. If she lays an egg in a chamber with two or three cicadas, that egg will produce a female. Nobody has yet unlocked the secret as to how the cicada killer knows she is laying a fertilized or unfertilized egg.

At any rate, the eggs hatch in two to three days. The larva then begins feeding on the paralyzed cicada. A larva will dine for about two weeks before it spins a cocoon that will house it until the next spring. When the cicada killer emerges from its silky cocoon, it is an adult.

A female cicada killer will construct several burrows, catch about 108 cicadas and lay some 24 male and 42 female eggs before she dies.

No adult cicada killers overwinter; all are dead by October. The insect's next generation is totally entrusted to the young developing below the ground.

As you might expect, cicada killers can inflict a painful sting. Luckily for us, though, they are rarely aggressive. In most instances, you have to actually pick one up for it to sting you.

If you are more than fifty years old, you probably know what a cicada killer is. Chances are you became acquainted with this giant wasp when you were a child. You are a member of a generation that grew up spending a lot of time outside when you were a youngster. Today, young people spend more time watching television and playing video games than playing outside. Consequently, they have never seen a cicada killer or many of the other animals with whom we share the world. I often wonder if this is indeed a sign of progress.

SUMMER IS CHIGGER TIME

I f you spend any time outdoors during the summer, you have probably had a bad experience with chiggers. You can't hide from them. They are found in gardens, on lawns, along hiking trails, or perched on vegetation growing along your favorite farm pond. By the time you realize that you have been attacked by these tiny creatures (each one-fiftieth of an inch long), many have already dropped off, leaving behind welts that just beg to be scratched.

The creature that causes us so much discomfort is a member of a large group of animals that includes such favorites as ticks, scorpions, and spiders. Like their relatives, adult chiggers have eight legs. Chiggers go by names such as harvest mites, red bugs, and furniture mites. While more than thirty thousand species of chiggers thrive throughout the world, only two species are a problem here.

Adult chiggers aren't the bad guys. They are typically red, are a bit larger than a period, and live in the ground, feeding on insects and their eggs.

Female chiggers are egg-laying machines. From spring through autumn, they lay a batch of up to four hundred eggs practically

112

every day. Eggs are most often laid on damp soil, and about a week after they are laid, they hatch into tiny larvae. Unlike their parents, the youngsters have six legs and are so small that five could sit side by side atop a period. The only way these tiny animals can become adults is by feeding on flesh. In order to better their chances of finding a suitable meal, these parasites slowly make their way to the tip of a blade of grass or branch. Here, they wait until an unsuspecting animal happens by. Whenever the victim brushes against the vegetation on which the chiggers are perched, the parasites try to latch on to the passing animal. More often than not, the chigger larvae attach themselves to rodents, birds, snakes, turtles, and toads. However, as far as we are concerned, too often we are the hapless victims.

Since chiggers are so small, and because we are often unable to feel them walking about on our skin, we often don't realize we are playing host to them until red, itchy welts begin popping up to eight hours later.

At that point, if we are fortunate, we will have only a few bites to contend with. However, some people experience hundreds of bites. The reason for this is that chigger eggs are laid in large groups.

If we are unlucky and run into a horde of hungry chigger larvae, the chiggers immediately begin moving about on our skin, searching for a place to feed. They seem to prefer feeding in a confined spot such as within armpits, behind the knees, or around waistbands or socks.

Contrary to popular belief, chiggers don't burrow into the skin. Instead, they insert their piercing mouthparts into our skin. The parasites then inject some chemicals that prevent our blood from clotting and literally digest our flesh. The chigger subsequently sucks up its liquid meal. If left undisturbed, chiggers will feed for three to four days before dropping off.

The intense itching that we associate with a chigger bite is caused by the tissue around the bite becoming liquefied. If that weren't enough, as it feeds, its droppings can cause infection at the site of the bite. Often the chigger that caused the welt and itching is no longer present when we begin to experience discomfort.

Should you happen to walk through areas that you suspect harbor chiggers, one of the things you can do to avoid a bout with intensely itchy chigger bites is to wipe your skin down with rubbing alcohol as soon as possible. Then when you get home, immediately take a bath or shower. While bathing, liberally soap your body several times. If any welts occur, treat the wounds with an antiseptic and a nonprescription anesthetic. Some folks report that meat tenderizer rubbed on a bite helps stop the itching.

Ideally, you should try to prevent chiggers from ever reaching your skin. This is best accomplished by wearing long pants and long-sleeved shirts. Tuck your pant cuffs into your boots or socks, and then spray your clothing with an insect repellent containing DEET.

Don't let chiggers ruin a summer outing. By taking the proper precautions, you can ward off an onslaught of chiggers and have a super time enjoying the Monroe County outdoors.

PART 4

Mammals

FOX SQUIRRELS—THE FORGOTTEN ONES

G ray squirrels are common sights throughout Monroe County. They can be seen in backyards and woodlands alike. In fact, it would be safe to say they are the most commonly seen wild mammals in the county. Consequently, it is easy to forget that the gray squirrel's close relative, the fox squirrel, also makes its home here.

Most Monroe Countians don't see even one fox squirrel a year. When one is spotted, it is a memorable experience. Therefore, you can imagine Eunice Wilkerson's surprise when a fox squirrel began making her backyard a regular stop on its daily travels. Eunice describes the animal as being the biggest and most colorful squirrel she has ever seen. While Eunice has feeders stocked with seed, the squirrel prefers to search for hidden nuts and fungi when it visits her yard.

A few years ago, while escorting a couple from England around the Rum Creek Wildlife Management Area looking for birds, we happened upon a fox squirrel standing on its hind legs beside the road. After watching the squirrel for several minutes, the lady from England told me that seeing the squirrel was the highlight of their trip.

Indeed, the fox squirrel is a striking animal. Fox squirrels are up to 20 percent larger than the gray squirrels. A large fox squirrel will tip the scales at three pounds in weight.

It has often been said that no two fox squirrels look alike. From my experiences, I would have to say that is probably the case. These large squirrels have three color phases. In the western portion of its range (Colorado, east Texas, and the Dakotas), most fox squirrels sport gray backs and bright rust-colored hair on their undersides. In the Northeast, the majority of fox squirrels are predominantly grayish with yellow bellies. Here in Georgia and the rest of the Southeast, they are most commonly black and sport white-tipped tails and white blazes on their faces.

You might wonder where the fox squirrel got its name. This large squirrel was so named because its coat looks much like the red-and-gray coat of our native gray fox.

Fox squirrels prefer to live in open, mature pine, oak/hickory, and live oak forests. They are one of the key wildlife inhabitants of the longleaf pine forests of south Georgia.

They eat a variety of foods. While they will occasionally dine on a bird egg or hatchling, frogs, insects, and even dead fish, they feed primarily on acorns, hickory nuts, buds, fruits, the inner bark of trees, mulberries, walnuts, poplar fruit, hawthorn seeds, buds, and green pinecones. They are also fond of a type of fungus that grows beneath the ground. Fox squirrels locate the tasty fungus by smell, much like certain hogs that are able to locate valuable truffles. When the squirrels eat the subterranean treats, they consume the plant's spores. These spores are spread throughout the forest in the squirrels' droppings. This is of great value to the forests, as the fungi help valuable forest trees geminate and encourage the growth of nitrogen-fixing bacteria.

Like other squirrels, fox squirrels bury nuts. In fact, fox squirrels have been known to bury several thousand nuts in only three months' time.

Depending on the availability of food and den sites, the fox squirrel's home range varies anywhere from ten to fifty acres in size. Typically, females have smaller home ranges than males.

Since fox squirrels can roam over a large area, you might not see one of these large squirrels using your property. A sure sign that fox squirrels have been around is the presence of what appear to be neatly trimmed twigs littering the ground beneath tall trees. The twigs are lopped off by these squirrels as they sharpen their teeth.

Since fox squirrels sweat through the bottoms of their feet, during hot weather the squirrels will sometimes leave wet tracks on rocks and other smooth surfaces.

Fox squirrels have two litters of two to four young twice a year. The first litter is born in late winter or early spring. A second litter arrives in the summer.

Fox squirrels prefer to nest in tree cavities. However, if no cavities exist, they will build and use leaf nests. These leafy bowers are often constructed in the crotches of trees. It is not unusual for a squirrel to use three to six nests.

If you are lucky enough to have fox squirrels on your property, here are a few things you can do to help them out:

- Retain cavity- and nut-producing trees.
- Erect fox-squirrel nesting boxes where cavity trees are missing or in short supply.
- Routinely burn and thin pine woodlands to maintain open, parklike stands.

Sadly, fox squirrels have proven that they aren't very adaptable to our uses of the land. Consequently, throughout much of their range, particularly in the Southeast, fox-squirrel populations are declining. Therefore, if we are to continue to enjoy this remarkable animal, we must restore fox-squirrel habitat when it has been destroyed and better maintain what habitat remains.

THE WHITETAIL'S COOL SUMMER COAT

Would you think of wearing a thick, fleece-lined jacket in July or a pair of shorts on a cold winter day? I don't think so. You dress in the clothes that are appropriate for the season. Such is also the case with Monroe County's favorite game animal—the white-tailed deer.

If you live in Monroe County, you get to see lots of deer. However, if you do more than give a deer a passing glance, you have probably noticed that the deer you see dining in your garden or standing in a roadside field are a different color than the deer you saw this past winter. If you did, you saw whitetails bedecked in their new summer duds.

From a distance, the whitetail's winter coat looks grayish brown. On closer examination, the vast majority of these hairs have reddish-brown tips. Others are tipped with black. This coat is very thick and is actually composed of two distinctly different types of hair. The long outer hairs (guard hairs) are very long, brittle, and hollow. They are also waterproof. Beneath them is a thick layer of extremely fine, soft hairs. These hairs are quite wooly and help the

deer retain body heat. This natural insulation is extremely important to a deer trying to keep warm in frigid winter weather.

Several weeks ago, while we were enjoying the beauty of early
spring flowers, and winter was slowly giving way to spring, white-
tailed deer began losing their heavy winter coats. The hair often
falls off in big chunks, giving them a ragged, almost mangy look.
As they continue to lose their winter pelage, you begin to realize
just how thick the winter coat was. When the process is completed,
deer appear considerably thinner than a few weeks before—just as
we do after we take off a bulky winter coat. They will wear this new
coat for the next three months—the hottest months of the year.

The new guard hairs are wiry, fewer in number, up to two inches shorter, and not hollow. They also lack black pigment and are
therefore lighter in color. This thinner, light-colored coat helps the
deer keep cool. The thick inner coat is shed further, adding to the
comfort of the deer during the hot summer.

This is extremely advantageous, because deer have very few
sweat glands. When sweat evaporates on the skin, it has a cooling
affect. As a result, aside from a thin, light-colored coat, deer can
only alleviate body heat by panting.

Regardless of the season, it is important that a deer's coat be as
waterproof as possible. Waterproofing is provided in large part by
water-repellent oil produced by glands in the deer's skin. Once on
the animal's skin, the oil eventually coats the deer's hair, making
it waterproof.

Fawns are dressed for summer. They are covered with a reddish-brown coat festooned with white spots. This combination offers the young deer excellent camouflage. When a fawn is lying on
the ground, its spots and brown pelage blend in perfectly with the
sun-dappled ground.

With the approach of winter, whitetails, including those born
in the spring, begin losing their reddish coats as they prepare for
the harsh winter months. In fact, the transformation can begin as

early as August or September. The length of time it takes a deer to shed its summer coat and replace it with its winter pelage is related to the health of the animal. The process is much shorter in healthy deer.

This fall, when you are headed to a football game on a crisp evening and dressed in a sweater and slacks, the deer you see running across the road in front of your car will also be appropriately dressed—in its new, grayish-brown winter coat.

OUR FASCINATION WITH ANTLERS

We have a fascination with antlers. We hang them on the walls of our homes and even mount them on the hoods of our hunting vehicles. We use them to adorn knives, jewelry, pistol grips, and buttons. Some suggest that they have magical powers. Others claim they can cure everything from anemia to hypertension and snake bites.

Each fall, thousands of men and women eagerly anticipate the opening of the deer-hunting season. At this magical time of the year, they renew their quest to bag a buck with a better rack than any they have ever taken before.

Nonhunters scratch their heads as they try to understand why these specialized bones captivate our thoughts and dreams. While deer hunters can't explain their compulsion, they know it is as real as a steaming cup of coffee cooked over a crackling campfire.

The more you learn about antlers, the easier it is to appreciate why they are so special.

Mammologists tell us that animals with antlers have been around for some twenty-five million years. Today, all members of the true deer family have antlers. In North America, this family is represented by the white-tailed deer, mule deer, elk, moose, and caribou. The males of all of these game animals display bony growths atop their heads called antlers. With the exception of the caribou, the females of these species only rarely sport antlers.

Most experts feel that antlers are used by male deer during head-butting bouts to resolve breeding and territorial contests. While many biologists believe that bucks with the largest antlers have an advantage over those with smaller racks, others suggest that body weight plays a bigger role in determining the victor in these disputes.

Although animals like cows retain their horns throughout their lives, antlers are shed annually. Locally, bucks begin dropping their antlers in January. Antler shedding is triggered by day length. Typically, larger bucks will shed their racks before smaller bucks. In fact, smaller bucks may retain their antlers up to two months longer than their bigger brothers.

Bucks begin growing a new set of antlers by mid-March, and growth continues until August or early September. While an antler is growing, it is covered with a soft, prickly material called velvet. The velvet contains nerves and a myriad of blood vessels which supply the growing antler with nutrients.

Developing antlers are among the fastest-growing tissues known to man. It is common for an antler to grow a half inch per day. This phenomenal growth rate has piqued the interest of medical researchers, who are studying antler growth in hopes of better understanding the growth of cancer cells.

As antlers cease growing, their velvet covering dries and is rubbed off on the limbs and trunks of small trees. Generally speaking, the bigger the buck, the larger the tree it uses to rub off the velvet. While most velvet is rubbed off within a day, shreds of it will often remain on the antlers for several weeks.

It is difficult to find velvet in the woods. Most hunters have never found any. One reason for this is that some bucks will actually eat their own velvet.

The size and shape of a set of antlers are determined by heredity, age, and food. One of the most common questions posed by deer hunters is "Why don't I see more trophy deer?" The answer is actually quite simple. The primary reason more monster bucks aren't seen locally is that bucks rarely live long enough to develop a decent rack. In Monroe County, most bucks don't live to see their second birthday. More than 60 percent of the adult bucks bagged in middle Georgia are only one and a half years old when harvested. A buck needs to reach at least three and a half or more years of age before it develops a true trophy rack. In most counties, it is not uncommon to find that only 2 percent of the antlered bucks are four and a half years old or older when they are bagged.

A buck has a high demand for protein, calcium, and phosphorus during the spring and summer when its antlers are growing. During drought years, the nutritive value of deer browse decreases. This can result in antlers being smaller than they would be during a normal year. The rainfall the county received this past summer should have helped bucks grow bigger antlers this year than they have for a quite a while.

In spite of the fact that most of us will not see, let alone bag, a trophy buck this season, our optimism remains high. You never know when the next deer that walks past your tree stand is that trophy you have been waiting a lifetime to see. The rest is up to you.

THE RUT

Whenever deer hunters gather around the campfire on a crisp fall evening, sooner or later the subject of the rut will come up. The reason for this is simple—during the peak of the rut, hunters have perhaps their best chance of bagging a buck. With that in mind, you need to know that the peak of the rut in Monroe County is occurring right now!

A lot of theories exist about what triggers the rut. One of the most widely held is that the peak of the rut takes place a week after the second full moon after the autumn equinox. As such, this is called the rutting moon. A number of studies, however, including one conducted by the University of Georgia, have found that there doesn't seem to be any relationship between the moon and the peak of the rut.

While wildlife biologists aren't sure why the peak of the rut varies across the state and country, all agree that the onset of the rut is sparked by decreasing day length. Consequently, weeks before the Monroe County landscape is decorated with a tapestry of red, yellow, and orange leaves, bucks begin going into rut.

A buck beginning to shed velvet from its antlers is one of the most easily recognizable signs that the rut has begun. During this time, look for pieces of velvet hanging from bushes and trees that the buck has used in an attempt to it rub off.

Once the velvet is shed, bucks begin entering into pushing contests with one another. Such confrontations are not fights—the bucks simply lock antlers and try to push each other backward. Sooner or later, one buck will break off the sparring and both animals will begin feeding. These contests determine who is dominant and will have the best chance of breeding the does in that neck of the woods.

As the rut progresses, the bucks' necks begin to swell as they reach peak physical condition. They begin rubbing their antlers on trees and making scrapes using their front feet, scratching all of the vegetation and leaves from an area roughly three feet in diameter. They will then urinate on the exposed earth. The vast majority of scrapes are made beneath a branch some four and a half to five feet above the ground. The bucks hook and rub their heads on the overhanging branches, often twisting or breaking the boughs.

Some four to six weeks before the onset of the rut, bucks begin chasing does. At first, they will pursue them at a distance of 160 feet or more. During the time when a buck is trailing a doe, he will often grunt, his nose to the ground, while holding his tail straight out. Should he attempt to get too close to a doe, she will quickly dart away.

The does eventually allow the bucks to approach more closely. This coincides with the bucks' becoming less tolerant of one another. If a younger buck happens across an older buck trailing doe, he will often join the chase. However, he will stay well back from the dominant buck. During the three-week rutting period, bucks will often fight with one another. As a general rule, mature bucks won't fight with a younger buck. When fights do occur, they typically take place between bucks that are of roughly equal size. One buck will charge his opponent from three to six feet away. His attack will be directed at the other's antlers.

Some two days before a doe is ready to breed, she will actually seek out a buck. Once a buck and a receptive doe locate one another, they are inseparable during the day prior to breeding as well as the day breeding actually takes place. If, however, a doe is not able to breed on the day she is receptive, she will be ready to breed again in twenty-eight days. In some instances, does may go through three to four cycles before they are bred. A buck, on the other hand, may breed four to twenty does during his rut.

The rut puts terrific strain on bucks. During this time, a mature buck may lose 25 to 35 percent of his body weight. As the rut wanes, the buck's swollen neck shrinks, and he loses interest in the does.

The reason bucks are more vulnerable to hunters during the rut is that they travel much more widely than normal, looking for does willing to mate with them. Meanwhile, they are much less wary than normal. Their carelessness and constant roaming can be their undoing. Some recklessly dart out into highways, colliding with cars and trucks. Others are harvested by hunters that have been patiently waiting silently for a buck to pass their way.

The peak of the rut in Monroe County takes place in the second week of November. With that in mind, you might want to spend a little extra time in the woods during the next week or so. If you do, you might be rewarded with a freezer full of venison and a trophy for your wall.

Good luck!

OPOSSUM AND SWEET POTATOES, ANYONE?

Practically all Monroe Countians can identify an opossum. While it is one of the most common game mammals found in Monroe County, most of us don't really don't know much about them. Until armadillos invaded the county, they were the most common animals seen dead on our highways. We know that they are slow moving. Some of the older folks among us know that the most famous of all opossums is an opossum named Pogo that lives in the Okefenokee Swamp in south Georgia. Pogo was the star of the late Walt Kelly's popular comic strip that ran from 1948 to 1975.

I must admit that even though I am a wildlife biologist, I don't know as much as I should about this animal. When I was in college, my professors spent little time discussing the life history and habitat needs of this nocturnal game animal with us budding wildlife biologists. They chose instead to spend precious class time teaching us about ducks, geese, white-tailed deer, quail, doves, turkeys, and other more glamorous game animals.

I am a firm believer that to really get to know a wild animal, you need to see it in the wild. Well, I recently went eye to eye with a wild opossum, and I and the folks with me came away with a new understanding of this curious animal.

Our encounter with an opossum was a classic case of serendipity. On the Saturday afternoon after a recent snowstorm, my wife, Donna, granddaughter, Anna, and I went into town for supper. As we returned home at dusk, just as I was turning into the garage, my wife spotted an opossum eating a baked sweet potato I had tossed into the butterfly garden for mulch. Before I could park the car, the opossum disappeared into a small strip of trees that separate my property from the backyard of our neighbors Ann Chidre and Jimmy Stephens.

I ran into the house, grabbed my camera, and returned to the scene. Anna and I looked for the opossum for a few minutes but without success. We were just about to end our search when I spotted it. In the gathering darkness, it was perched motionless on the side of a small hardwood tree no more than five and a half feet above the ground. Its salt-and-pepper-colored fur blended perfectly with the mottled gray bark of the trees. In fact, I doubt I would have seen had its plump body not protruded well beyond the slender trunk of the tree.

Anna raced into the house to tell her granny that we had found the opossum, and I began to take pictures. Once my granddaughter returned with my wife in tow, I moved closer. When I approached within six feet on the animal, it began to slowly slide down the slippery bark of the tree. Only then did it move—it tried to shimmy back up the tree. It would make a little headway and then slip back and try again. It was forced to repeat this process several times. Finally, it returned to the spot it had occupied when I found it. It appeared the small tree's trunk tapered just enough at that point to prevent the animal from going any higher.

Although opossums will often hiss, salivate, and bare their teeth when they feel threatened by a potential predator, this 'possum never did. By the same token, it didn't "played dead" either. While we often read about opossums using this ruse to avoid harm, the truth that is they rarely do. This animal relied totally on its camouflage and ability to remain motionless to avoid detection.

We called Jimmy and Ann down to see what we had found. There we were, five people within but a few feet of the opossum, and it didn't move. All of us were eye to eye with a wild opossum.

This provided us with the unique opportunity to closely study this unusual critter for as long as we wanted. While the opossum had a mouthful of teeth—fifty, to be exact—the only ones we saw were its upper canines, one protruding from its upper lip on either side of its head. We got a close look at its thick, whitish, bare tail. Its head was white, and its nose was light pink and not pointed as it always seems to be depicted in cartoons. It was actually flattened and looked piglike. Its ears were black and bordered with white, flattened, and seemingly about the thickness of a thick potato chip.

To me, its most fascinating features were its pink feet. Its front feet looked much like the front feet of a squirrel. In comparison, its hind feet resembled a human hand. Each digit, except the thumb, was armed with a nail.

With night quickly coming on, we decided to leave the opossum on the side of the tree. When I returned about an hour later, it was gone.

That afternoon, each of us learned a lot about opossums and came away with a greater appreciation for this often maligned critter. When the opossum left to go about its nightly search for food, it left each of us a lasting memory of our encounter with a wild animal in its natural habitat. Additionally, I returned to the house convinced that having a sweet-potato-eating opossum is far better than eating opossum baked with sweet potatoes.

PART 5

Plants

ZINNIAS AND I GO BACK A LONG WAY

O ut of all the plants my wife and I grow to enhance the beauty of our property and provide wildlife with food, none has a more personal meaning to me than the zinnia.

My mother introduced me to this garden favorite when I was a youngster. I can remember the folks who manufactured the laundry detergent Oxydol offering their customers seed packets. As I recall, all you had to do was send in so many Oxydol box tops and a small amount of money, and you would receive packets containing the seeds of zinnias and other popular garden flowers.

My mother responded to the promotion one winter, and several weeks later, the seeds arrived in the mail.

By the time spring finally arrived and the garden was tilled, I had forgotten all about the flower seeds until one morning my mom asked my brother and me, "Boys, do you want to plant the flower garden today?" We answered in the affirmative and followed her to the garden.

My mother dug a shallow furrow and showed us how to scatter the seeds. Following her example as best we could, we dropped the seeds into the moist, dark soil. She followed behind and covered them with gentle strokes of her hoe and then tamped the dirt down with its flat front side. Then it was time to wait.

When summer arrived and I was spending my days fishing, playing baseball, swimming, and mowing the grass, the flowers began blooming. For the life of me, I can't remember the names of any of the flowers we planted—except the zinnias. They were something to behold. Their red, orange, yellow, and white blossoms seemed to vie with each other to catch our attention. I must admit I don't remember butterflies visiting the flowers, although I am sure they did. What I do recall is vainly trying to catch a hummingbird in a glass mayonnaise jar as the tiny bird fed on the zinnia flowers' nectar.

Now that I am a lot older and a little wiser, I still plant zinnias. I haven't lost my fondness for their beauty. However, I now plant them as much for the wildlife they draw to my yard as for their attractiveness.

Zinnias are one of the easiest flowers you can grow for wildlife. As I discovered years ago, hummingbirds love 'em. And as anyone who has ever planted zinnias can attest, they are also a favorite with butterflies. On a sunny, hot summer day, it is next to impossible to look at a patch of zinnias and not see a bevy of beautiful butterflies. The list of butterflies that visit my garden includes swallowtails like the eastern tiger, black, pipevine, and spicebush, American and painted ladies, fiery, clouded, and ocola skippers, to name a few.

I also see lots of other nectar feeders feeding at the showy flowers, including native solitary bees. I have even spotted moths visiting the blossoms at night.

One thing I have also discovered is that the seeds are a favorite of the American goldfinch. I have watched goldfinches perch atop the withered heads of zinnia flowers and pluck out seeds one by one. Other birds that also dine on the seeds are chipping sparrows and Carolina chickadees.

Zinnias come in a wide range of colors and sizes. Some grow only about six inches tall while others soar to four feet or more in height. Zinnia flowers range from red to white. In fact, about the only colors you cannot get them in are blue and black.

I have found that butterflies and hummingbirds prefer flat, single-flowered varieties over those that are round or double flowered.

You don't need to be in a hurry to plant zinnia seeds, because they don't do well when temperatures hover below fifty degrees Fahrenheit. As such, they are among the last seeds I plant each spring.

Zinnias will do well in any location that receives at least six hours of direct sunlight a day. However, if you are planting zinnias with butterflies in mind, locate the planting in a spot that is protected from strong breezes. Although the plants do remarkably well without a lot of water, it has been my experience that they will wilt when the soil in my garden dries out a bit.

You don't even have to have a garden spot to enjoy zinnias. The smaller varieties of zinnias also do well in containers that can be placed along walkways or on patios, decks, and porches.

One of the things I like best about zinnias is that if I deadhead the spent blooms, the plants will continue to bear flowers throughout the summer. However, along about mid- to late September, I begin letting the plants go to seed. That is when the goldfinches show up. I also let the dead zinnia stalks stand throughout the fall and winter, as birds will dine on the brown seed heads and any seeds that have fallen onto the ground.

When searching for new flowers to add to your landscape, don't forget to consider old standbys such as zinnias. These time-tested backyard favorites rarely disappoint.

Whenever I am planting a bed of zinnias, as the seeds sift through my fingers, my mind is flooded with fond memories of my childhood and a mother that took the time to introduce me to a plant that I have enjoyed for a lifetime. Indeed, zinnias and I go back a long way.

March 25, 2015

REDBUDS ARE STEALING THE SHOW

One of the things I enjoy most about spring in Monroe County is that at that special time of the year, we are treated to Mother Nature's annual parade of wildflowers. This special event begins well before the Forsythia Festival and extends well into May. Like the bands, floats, and marchers in a parade, each of our wildflowers appears across the countryside in an ordered sequence. During the past week, one of the first native flowering trees to appear along the parade route that stretches from Bolingbroke to High Falls has been the eastern redbud.

The redbud is one of the smaller native trees found in Monroe County. Indeed, a forty-foot redbud is considered a giant. Most mature redbuds are actually much smaller in size.

If you would like to take a gander at the tree the Georgia Forestry Commission has certified as the Georgia champion redbud, you do not have far to go. The tree holding this title has its roots sunk in the soil just beyond the parking lot behind the United Bank in downtown Forsyth.

The redbud has attractive foliage. Its three- to five-inch leaves are heart shaped. In autumn, these leaves turn yellow-green.

The tree produces long, flat, green seedpods that remind me of Kentucky Wonder pole beans. These pods turn brown to purple in the autumn.

While the color provided by the tree's foliage and seedpods is pleasing to the eye, it does not compare to the floral show provided by its flowers in early spring. These half-inch blossoms are shaped much like English pea blooms. Their color can best be described as rosy pink or reddish purple. The blossoms are arranged in clusters on year-old twigs and even the tree's trunk.

Eastern redbuds bloom before the leaves appear on most trees. As such, they bring a splash of spring color to our often otherwise bleak landscape.

If you are like me, you have probably often wondered where the redbud got its name. The tree is supposedly named for the color of its unopened buds. While I will admit these buds are often dark pink, I think it is a stretch to say they are red.

Odder still is the fact that the redbud is sometimes called the Judas tree. According to Christian legend, after Judas Iscariot betrayed Jesus, he hanged himself on a redbud tree. Prior to that time, the tree's blossoms were supposedly white. However, ever since the death of Christ's betrayer, they are red with blood and shame.

The redbud provides food for a variety of wild animals, although it is not nearly as important a food plant as oaks, dogwoods, and some of our other native trees. Its seeds are eaten by birds, including cardinals, rose-breasted grosbeaks, quail, and wild turkeys. Both deer and squirrels will also dine on the seeds, and the leaves of young redbuds are browsed by white-tailed deer.

That being said, in late winter and early spring, redbud blossoms are an important source of pollen and/or nectar and are eaten by a number of creatures, such as bees, moths, butterflies, and ruby-throated hummingbirds.

The only butterfly known to use the redbud as a host plant is the small (seven-eighths of an inch to one and one-eighth inches) grayish-brown Henry's elfin.

However, it is the host of a small number of moths, including the strikingly beautiful Io moth.

In the wild, redbuds are considered to be an understory tree. In other words, they prosper in the partial shade found beneath the canopy of much larger trees. However, it will also grow in open sites.

While the tree does well in rich, moist soil types, it can also be found growing in dry sites.

These attributes, along with its small size, make the redbud a great tree to plant in most yards. Not surprisingly, therefore, it can be seen growing in cities, suburban, and rural yards.

When planted in an open yard, the tree will sometimes spread out up to thirty feet. The trunk's habit of dividing close to the ground helps create a supersmall shade tree.

If planted in partial shade, homeowners will be rewarded with delightful spring color at a time of year when apart from daffodils and forsythias, most yards are devoid of flowers.

Redbud trees are easy to grow and can be purchased at many nurseries. In addition, since the tree's seeds readily germinate, if you look around the base of a redbud, you can often find an abundance of seedlings ready for transplanting. As such, it is an ideal pass-along plant.

Also, since the tree blooms when it is only four or five years old, you won't have to wait very long to enjoy its color.

For the next couple of weeks, we can sit back and enjoy the redbud's beauty. However, as is the case with all spring flowers, their time for marching past the Monroe County viewing stand will then pass as the parade marches on toward summer. Then it will be time to get ready for the next batch of flowers to appear along our local parade route. One of the most notable of these is the flowering dogwood. Isn't spring great?

FLOWERING DOGWOOD—A FAVORITE WITH MAN AND WILDLIFE

The flowering dogwood is arguably the most beautiful native tree in North America. In the spring, this small tree decorates our yards and woodlands with banks of creamy-white blossoms. In fall, its foliage turns scarlet and, together with its bright red berries, seemingly lights up the autumn landscape. If its beauty were not enough to endear it to us, the flowering dogwood is also one of our most valuable wildlife food plants. Its berries and foliage are eaten by more than one hundred species of birds and mammals.

We may never know for certain why this flowering tree is called dogwood. Legends tell us that it earned its name from a medicine concocted from its bark that was once used to treat dogs suffering from the mange. Others suggest that the name *dogwood* is a derivation of the word *daggerwood*. At one time, daggerwood sticks were sharpened and used to skewer meat for cooking.

Christian legends claim that wood from a dogwood tree was used to make the cross on which Jesus Christ was crucified. It is said that at that time, dogwood trees were as massive as any of the largest oaks. As Jesus hung on the cross, he could sense that the dogwood used to make the cross felt ashamed that the tree had been used for such a horrible purpose. It is purported that Christ told the tree that henceforth no dogwood would ever again grow large enough to be used to create a cross and that as a reminder of his suffering, dogwood flowers would forever more form a cross with two long and two short petals. At the edge of each petal would be found brownish areas that look much like rusty nail prints. In addition, a crown of thorns would be situated at the middle of the flower.

Some 110 species of dogwood exist around the world. Most of the trees are native to Europe, North America, and Asia. The flowering dogwood occurs naturally from southern Maine westward to eastern Kansas and south into Florida. In Georgia, it is grows in all of our 159 counties.

The flowering dogwood lives in a wide range of habitats. It can be found rooted in a variety of soil types but does best in rich, well-drained, acidic soils. While it grows in open sun and can withstand temperatures up to 115 degrees Fahrenheit, it prefers partial shade. Although it will survive in heavy shade, it rarely blooms there.

In the wild, flowering dogwoods can be found growing in the forest understory, beneath the canopy formed by pines, oaks, and other taller trees. Consequently, they remain hidden through much of the year.

However, in the spring, before most of the leaves have emerged on hardwood trees, flowering dogwoods announce their presence with a flood of creamy-white blossoms. One of the best places to view this floral show is along the Little Rock Wildlife Drive located on the Piedmont National Wildlife Refuge in Jones County. During the peak of the dogwood blooming season, the blossoms seemingly form white clouds suspended beneath a dark-green canopy of pines.

After the flowers have withered and died, the dogwood trees once again blend into the landscape, only to reappear again in the fall. Then, as the days shorten and temperatures begin to drop, the flowering dogwood sets the middle Georgia woodlands ablaze with its scarlet foliage and shiny red berrylike fruits.

These nutrient-rich fruits are an important source of food for our wildlife neighbors from late summer into winter. Often, as you walk the autumn woodlands, you will find the fallen leaves beneath dogwoods trees scratched away by wild turkeys searching for fallen dogwood berries. While sitting silently in a deer stand, I have watched hermit thrushes pluck the bright-red berries from dogwood trees. Indeed, competition for the berries is keen. The list of birds and mammals that feed on dogwood berries includes quail, robins, mockingbirds, cardinals, woodpeckers, chipmunks, rabbits, and deer as well as gray and fox squirrels.

Although the value of the flowering dogwood as an extremely important wildlife food plant is undisputed, its future is uncertain. A deadly anthracnose fungus has killed thousands of dogwoods in recent years. The disease has been especially devastating in north Georgia.

The flowering dogwood is a favorite with city, suburban, and rural homeowners. This small tree (twenty to thirty feet tall) is hardy, fast growing, attractive throughout the year, requires little care, and is resistant to insects. Also, its leaves decompose rapidly. Its ability to attract wildlife is a real bonus.

If you are planning to plant dogwoods on your property, don't transplant them from the wild, as they may be infected with the anthracnose virus. Instead, purchase disease-free trees from a reputable nursery. The Georgia Forestry Commission also sells bundles of bare root plants. Call your local Forestry Commission office for details.

In urban and suburban settings, dogwoods can be planted adjacent to roads and driveways as well as along the edges of yards.

They can even be used as specimen trees or scattered among widely spaced large trees.

In rural areas, where lacking, they should be planted in open woodlands. They also make great additions to fence rows and woodland borders.

Wherever they are found, they will add beauty to the landscape and provide a dependable source of food for a wide variety of wildlife. For the wildlife enthusiast, it doesn't get any better than that.

MULBERRIES—A FORGOTTEN TREAT

We Americans are fickle. We seem to jump from fad to fad. For a time, something like penny loafers or disco music will be the rage, only to fall out of favor and be forgotten a few years later. Take mulberries, for example. In the not-too-distant past, mulberry trees were found growing in backyards throughout the state. Additionally, since they make excellent shade trees, they were also planted in city parks and schoolyards.

My wife, Donna, recalls a particularly large mulberry tree that grew in the yard of her elementary school. During recess, she and her friends would dine on the sugary berries. After eating their fair share of the tasty treats, she and her classmates would return to class with red-stained fingers.

I can somewhat understand why mulberries have fallen out of favor. The berries will stain cement paths, clothes hanging on the line—in fact, just about any surface. Also, most of us have yards that are much smaller than those enjoyed by our parents and grandparents. Consequently, a single mulberry tree, which can soar thirty feet or more above the ground, is too large for the postage-stamp-sized backyards that are the norm today. Yet another side of me wonders why a tree that produces a bounty of tasty berries and is rated by the Cornell University Laboratory of Ornithology as one of the top seven most important plants for birds wouldn't be more popular with landowners.

Fortunately, my wife and I live on three acres of land, more than enough space to accommodate a large mulberry tree. Over the years, mulberry trees have popped up in a number of locations where birds have left their droppings containing mulberry seeds. However, until recently, none of these trees had produced any fruit. A few years ago, Donna discovered that one of the mulberry trees we had allowed to grow had produced a few one-and-a-half-to two-inch-long berries that looked much like blackberries. Each year since then, as the tree has grown larger, it has rewarded both us and our wildlife neighbors with more and more berries.

Our native mulberry is the red mulberry. The upper side of its leaves is hairy, and its fruits turn dark red. Male and female flowers can be found on the same or separate trees.

Another mulberry commonly found in Monroe County is the white mulberry, a native of Asia. White mulberry trees typically bear leaves whose upper sides are smooth. The berries of the white mulberry range in color from white to purplish red. Since white and red mulberry trees will hybridize, occasionally you will come across a mulberry tree whose identity will leave you scratching your head.

During the 1600s, the white mulberry and silk moths were brought into Georgia and elsewhere in the Southeast in an ill-fated attempt to launch the silk industry. The silkworm caterpillar feeds primarily on white mulberry leaves. These efforts were fostered by King James I. To further bolster the effort, in 1662 a law was passed mandating that every planter who didn't have at least ten mulberry trees for every hundred acres of land he owned would be fined ten pounds of tobacco. On the flip side, plantation owners that produced one thousand pounds of silk were granted bonuses of five thousand pounds of tobacco.

A mulberry tree festooned with a crop of juicy berries is next to impossible for wildlife to ignore. In fact, some fruit and berry growers will plant mulberries next to their orchards as decoy trees. They know that birds and other wildlife will often leave their crops alone and instead dine on the ripe mulberries.

More than five dozen species of birds alone eat mulberries. This long list includes quail, wild turkeys, indigo buntings, tanagers, catbirds, mockingbirds, brown thrashers, bluebirds, and great crested flycatchers, to name but a few. As many as twenty different species of birds have been seen dining at the same time in a single mulberry tree. Deer and raccoons, even opossums and chipmunks, also partake in the sugary berries. Mulberries are so important to squirrels that the planting of mulberries is often recommended to landowners wanting to manage their forests for bushytails.

If you are going to plant mulberry trees, I would recommend that you plant the native red mulberry, as its fruiting season is much longer than that of the white mulberry. In addition, many folks prefer the taste of red mulberries. It is one of Mother Nature's best health foods. A cup of the berries contains only sixty calories. The berries are rich in antioxidants, fiber, vitamins K and C, potassium, riboflavin, iron, magnesium, and potassium. Meanwhile, the berries also have a 10 percent sugar content and therefore can be used to make a variety of dishes, such as jams and jellies and an excellent wine—that is, if your wildlife neighbors are willing to share some berries with you.

If you have enough room, consider adding a red mulberry or two to your landscape. It might mean you will have to dry your Grateful Dead T-shirts in the dryer instead of the clothesline when the tree is fruiting, but this is a small price to pay for such a valuable tree.

THIS IS THE HONEYSUCKLE
YOU WANT IN YOUR BACKYARD

Recently, while walking to the mailbox early one morning, I spotted something red out of the corner of my eye. I turned and looked down at a cluster of bright-red tubular flowers blooming atop a mound of shiny, dark-green leaves. This splash of dazzling color was provided by a coral honeysuckle vine.

To many, the mere mention of the word *honeysuckle* conjures up the image of Japanese honeysuckle. As its name suggests, this is an alien plant first introduced into America in 1906. From its new home on Long Island, New York, during the twentieth century, this aggressive plant spread its vines across untold thousands of acres across the country.

As any Monroe Countian can attest, this despised plant seems to be everywhere. We find it growing in forests, along roadsides, in our shrubbery, in our gardens—you name it. It is indeed one of the bad guys of the plant world.

That being said, the coral honeysuckle, also known as trumpet honeysuckle and woodbine, is nothing like its reviled relative. I guess you can say that it is a gentle plant. It is not invasive, regales us with bouquets of gorgeous flowers for months on end, and is cloaked in attractive foliage throughout the year. In addition, is requires little or no care, is drought tolerant, and provides food and shelter for wildlife.

The coral honeysuckle is a native, semiwoody vine that grows from three to twenty feet in length. From late winter until frost, it bears an abundance of two-inch-long red, tubular-shaped flowers in four-inch clusters. However, the majority of the blooms are produced in spring and early summer. In this neck of the woods, it retains its shiny, purplish-green foliage throughout the year.

Although it grows best and displays the most blooms in slightly acidic, moist sites bathed in full sunlight, it will grow in a wide range of conditions. For example, I often find it growing in dry, red-clay soils as well as in both partial and complete shade.

When the plant doesn't have any support, it will trail along the ground or even form a small mound. However, when it is encouraged to climb something, like a trellis or a fence, its beauty takes on a new dimension.

One of the most spectacular plantings I have come across was located in Florida. The coral honeysuckle was growing on a wire fence in front of a home, creating a living wall of green foliage accented with splotches of stunning red flowers. As I stood admiring the plants, scores of hummingbirds drank nectar from the orange-tipped, tubular red blossoms.

One of the things I like best about coral honeysuckle is that it is a valuable wildlife plant. It is the host plant to two of my favorite insects. Both the spring azure butterfly and snowberry clearwing moth lay their eggs on the leaves of the plant. The spring azure is a dainty, powdery-blue butterfly that can be seen flitting about our yards at this time of the year. I am sure you have seen the snowberry clearwing—it is a day-flying moth that visits our flowers throughout the summer. Since it looks and acts like a tiny brown hummingbird, most folks call it the hummingbird moth.

A variety of nectar-feeders such as butterflies, moths and bees visit these flowers. It is a favorite nectar source of the ruby-throated hummingbird. Since it begins blooming in early spring, a time when nectar is scarce, it provides these backyard favorites with a source of food.

In late summer and fall, the vines are festooned with red or black berries. When these are ripe, a number of birds compete for them, including quail, both gold- and purple finches, and American robins.

It is easy to add coral honeysuckle to your landscape. Plants can be propagated from cuttings and seeds. In addition, seedlings are readily available at nurseries that deal in native plants. Although they may require a little tender, loving care when they are getting started, once established, they are practically maintenance-free.

I guarantee once you become familiar with coral honeysuckle, the name *honeysuckle* will take on a whole new meaning.

ROADSIDE ROYALTY

When you drive down any country road in the county right now, you are apt to spot scores of tall, white flowers growing along the roadsides, in ditches, and in nearby fields. These plants are popularly known as Queen Anne's lace.

Nobody knows who named this plant. However, one popularly held belief is that it was named for the wife of England's James I. It is known that she loved to embroider lace. Since the flower clusters displayed by this plant resemble fancy lace doilies, I guess centuries ago it seemed only natural to name the plant Queen Anne's lace. Legend has it that when Queen Anne pricked her finger with a needle while making a piece of fine lace, a drop of blood fell and dried on the lace. The purplish-black floret located near the center of each cluster of Queen Anne's lace flowers represents this drop of blood.

Since most of us have seen this attractive plant since we were children, it is perfectly logical to assume that it is native to North America. Such is not the case. Like so many of our plants, Queen Anne's lace is a foreign introduction.

Apparently, early colonists brought the plant to North America to adorn Victorian gardens. Since the plant spreads rapidly, it is now naturalized throughout most of the contiguous United States. In fact, it spreads so easily that it is sometimes called the devil's plague and may be found on the US Department of Agriculture's list of noxious weeds.

Queen Anne's lace is a biennial, which means that it lives for two years and doesn't produce flowers and reproduce until its second year of life.

The plant has fernlike leaves. Clusters of flowers (called umbels) adorn stems that can attain heights of twenty to eighty inches. The umbels are flat and can measure four inches or more across. Each flower cluster contains scores of tiny, white flowers. At times, these blossoms can also display a green or yellow tint. The centers of most of the umbels contain a single purplish flower. Botanists believe this special flower helps attract pollinating insects. The plant's taproot resembles a pale carrot. In fact, Queen Anne's lace is often called wild carrot.

These roots were once commonly eaten. By the same token, many folks have died after eating what they thought were the young, tender roots of the plant. This is because the plant looks remarkably like poison hemlock, which contains a deadly toxin. Consequently, I would recommend that you not eat the root or any other part of the plant.

That being said, Queen Anne's lace was eaten by the Romans, Europeans, and American colonists alike. Over the years, it has been served as a vegetable, used to sweeten pudding, and employed as a substitute for coffee. In fact, colonists even made wine from the roots. In addition, early Americans concocted a poultice from honey and leaves of Queen Anne's lace, using it to treat bacterial infections and sores. The colonists also made orange dye from the plant. Some two thousand years ago, none other than Hippocrates wrote that the plant's seeds could be used for birth control.

Nowadays, we recognize far different beneficial uses for this attractive plant. It is a little-known fact that it serves as a host for the black swallowtail butterfly. We are far more familiar with these large, yellow-spotted, green-and-black-banded caterpillars appearing on fennel, dill, and parsley plants.

In addition, Queen Anne's lace is a nectar plant. While butterflies such as red-banded hairstreaks feed on it, it is more often visited by native bees, wasps, and other nectar feeders.

This naturalized plant is showing up more often in wildflower gardens. This is principally because it blooms over a long period of time (upward of forty to sixty days), grows in a wide variety of soil types, needs little watering, and is easy to establish.

Both plants and seeds are available from nurseries. However, collecting and planting seeds from wild plants is easy and inexpensive.

At times, Queen Anne's lace will attempt to take over a garden. To prevent this from happening, clip off the plant's flowers soon after they go by. You can also manually pull the plants out of the ground.

If you would like to demonstrate to children how a plant absorbs water, place a freshly cut stem bearing an umbel into colored water. The flower will magically take on the color of the water.

A word of caution: when some folks touch Queen Anne's lace, their skin becomes irritated. With that in mind, make sure you are not allergic to the plant before touching it.

If you want to see her majesty during her annual visit to Monroe County, you had better do so soon. While the reign of the British royal family has lasted for centuries, her reign will end abruptly when the Department of Transportation and the Monroe County Highway Department mow the vegetation along our roads.

BEAUTYBERRY IS DESERVING OF ITS NAME

I have long thought that some of the names given wild animals and plants don't seem to fit. For example, I have never understood why a red-bellied woodpecker is called a red-bellied woodpecker when the only red on its belly is a light-reddish wash. To my way of thinking, the name red-necked woodpecker would be more appropriate since the bird's neck is bright red. I also believe the redbud was misnamed. Each spring when I gaze at a blooming redbud tree, for the life of me, I can't see how somebody years ago thought the tree's blossoms were red. The blooms are pink, not red.

Such is not the case with the American beautyberry. Indeed, take one look at the plant's bright purple berries, and you will have to agree that the berries are indeed beautiful. In addition, it is native to North America. The botanist that named this plant hit a home run!

I like beautyberries growing in my yard because not only are they indeed beautiful to look at, they are also eaten by some forty species of birds.

However, I must admit that the other day, I was not happy to see that a mockingbird had decided to make the beautyberry bush loaded with gorgeous berries near my office its own private dining spot. Why did it pick this bush when it could have chosen from several others scattered across my property? The reason for my irritation stems from the fact that while working one afternoon last week, I looked up and was astonished to see two adult male Baltimore orioles bedecked in bright orange and black plumage trying to drink nectar from my hummingbird feeder.

Before I could snap a picture of the breathtakingly beautiful birds, a mockingbird swooped in and almost hit the orioles. The orioles flew off, and a bit later, the feisty mockingbird resumed feeding on beautyberries. What luck! After years of waiting to see Baltimore orioles at my hummingbird feeder, their visit lasted mere seconds simply because a mockingbird didn't want to share nearby beautyberries with these long-distance migrants.

Some experts believe that the bright color of the beautyberries serves a very effective advertisement to migrants, much in the way we are lured off the highway with signs that say something like "All-you-can-eat buffet—$8.99." Like us, the migrating birds don't want to spend a long time dining. They have a long way to go, and the ability to easily find energy-rich food is advantageous to them.

You might be asking yourself, "How does this benefit the plant?" The answer is simple. Being easily spotted by wildlife increases the chances that the berries will be eaten. After the flesh of the berries is digested, the beautyberry's seeds are deposited some distance from the plant in the animals' droppings. Thus, the seeds are widely spread across the countryside and increase the plant's chance of survival. That's a pretty good trade-off.

While my resident mockingbird might have won this battle, I hate to tell him that his territorial battles have just begun. Before the last beautyberry is gobbled up, he will have to fend off other hungry migratory birds as well as permanent residents such as eastern towhees, catbirds, robins, thrushes, and our state bird, the brown thrasher. In addition, while the mockingbird is sleeping, chances are good that armadillos, raccoons, and even opossums might partake in some of the beautyberries.

One thing that makes the beautyberry such a great wildlife food plant is that its berries will remain on the plant well into winter. Consequently, if they aren't all eaten in late summer, they provide food for wild critters well into the time when fruits and berries are often hard to come by.

If you don't have American beautyberries growing in your yard, you need to plant some. The plant is hardy, will thrive in a variety of soil and light conditions, and requires little maintenance. In fact, about all you have to do is cut the plant back to within a few inches of the ground late in the winter.

If you get an American beautyberry or two started in your yard, it won't be long before you will be enjoying the sight of the shrub's attractive berries and the parade of birds drawn to this great native wildlife food plant. I am also convinced that you will agree with me—the American beautyberry is indeed worthy of its name.

NATURE'S CINDERELLA PLANT—STRAWBERRY BUSH

I n the children's classic story, *Cinderella*, an ordinary girl is magically transformed into a beautiful young woman by her fairy godmother. Mother Nature has her own version of Cinderella—it is the strawberry bush, and its eye-catching beauty can be enjoyed right now.

The strawberry bush is known by several unusual names. Some of these names are wahoo, burning bush, bursting heart, and hearts-a-busting. Regardless of what you call it, during the fall of the year, it is one of the most beautiful plants found in the woods.

Strawberry bush is a native deciduous shrub that prefers to grow in well-drained, acidic, fertile soils. It will grow in both uplands and lowlands but seems to prefer growing along streams.

This is one plant that will grow in the full shade. Here, growth is often slow and fruit production poor. The best sites are those bathed in partial shade.

Throughout much of the year, the strawberry bush is an unassuming plant. It grows anywhere from two to six feet tall. Throughout the spring and summer, it is cloaked in broad, lance-shaped, serrated green leaves that are borne on green stems and branches. The plant's modest flowers are light green and sometimes tinged with purple hues.

The seeds are produced within a one-inch, warty capsule that typically contains four to five berries. As the summer progresses, the green capsule grows larger and eventually turns red. While it is said this plant gets its name from the fact that these capsules look much like strawberries, I have always thought that both the color and shape of the mature capsules make them appear more like raspberries.

Sometime in September or October, the capsules split open, revealing scarlet berries suspended on threadlike structures. The appearance of the open capsule and red berries accounts for the variation of the plant's name hearts-a-bursting.

As summer begins giving way to fall, the leaves begin turning a bright red. The combination of the strawberry bush's unusual scarlet fruit and stunning red leaves catches the eye of the most casual observer. Once you have seen the plant, you can't help but be smitten by its breathtaking beauty.

Deer are so fond of strawberry bush that it is often referred to as deer ice cream. In fact, they can't seem to get enough to the plant's foliage and stems. Consequently, it is one of the first woodland plants to disappear when deer populations are high. For that reason, this plant is often difficult to find growing wild in Monroe County. As soon as it sprouts, deer eat it. Strangely, it has been reported that the plant is poisonous to both cattle and sheep.

Fortunately, it isn't poisonous to other forms of wildlife. Rabbits will browse on strawberry bush leaves and branches. Birds such as the wild turkey, yellow-rumped warbler, eastern bluebird, wood thrush, and northern mockingbird eat the shrub's red berries. For that reason, while the seeds will persist well into winter, they often disappear well before Christmas.

Early colonists found the plant so beautiful that as early as 1663, it became one of the first North American plants sent back to Europe for use in ornamental gardens.

Long before the first Europeans set foot in the New World, however, Native Americans believed that the strawberry bush had great therapeutic value. It is said that they used the roots of the plant to concoct a tea to treat maladies of both the urinary tract and the stomach. Later, various parts of the plant were used to treat dandruff, constipation, malaria, and liver problems.

The strawberry bush's bark and fruit should never be eaten, as some experts report that chemicals contained within them may result in cardiac arrest and severe diarrhea.

Strawberry bush is an ideal plant for home landscapes. Plants can also be propagated from seeds. However, since seeds are very difficult to germinate, requiring specialized treatments that last for months, I don't recommend that you try to obtain plants for home plantings in this manner. Root clumps are much easier to deal with. They can be successfully transplanted in winter.

However, I recommend that you do not remove any plants from the wild unless you are rescuing them from an area that will be bulldozed. You are much better off buying plants from nurseries specializing in native plants.

When you begin planning additions to your home landscape, put the strawberry bush on your list. Once you get Mother Nature's Cinderella growing in your backyard, it will soon transform your backyard into a fantasy of fall color.

October 14, 1998

A PRELUDE TO THE MAIN SHOW

Weeks before the kaleidoscope of colorful fall foliage takes center stage throughout the state, we are treated with another visually spectacular show. This floral tapestry is fashioned with plumes of gold waving enticingly from roadside ditches, old fields, and even along the edges of backyards such as mine.

Like far too many of our wild plants, goldenrod is largely unappreciated by most Georgians. In fact, many who suffer from allergies often blame their stuffy noses and watery eyes on this lovely plant. In truth, goldenrod pollen is rarely the cause of their malady. Only about one to two percent of the pollen floating about when goldenrod is blooming is produced by this showy plant. Actually, ragweed, which is also blooming then, is often the culprit. However, since the ragweed's flowers are drab and inconspicuous, its blossoms are rarely noticed by allergy sufferers. Ragweed is wind pollinated while goldenrod pollen is quite heavy and sticky. Consequently, it is spread from place to place primarily by insects and not the fall breezes.

In fact, while it is blooming, untold numbers of nectar feeders such as moths, butterflies, bumblebees, wasps, soldier beetles, honeybees, syrphid flies, and others converge on the plant's breathtaking floral displays. These unknowing pollinators are there to reap their share of the goldenrod's pollen and/or nectar.

As often happens, what is a weed to some is a valued landscape plant to others. While goldenrod is often featured in gardens throughout Europe, only now is it beginning to take a well-deserved place in American gardens. I am sure that it will eventually prove to be a garden favorite, as this perennial is hardy and requires little care. Additionally, these wildflowers rarely need staking and often take on a more pleasing shape when grown in gardens.

Perhaps the easiest way to establish goldenrod is by dividing the rhizomes of mature plants in the early spring. A large goldenrod plant can be broken into two dozen or more pieces. This can be done every three to four years without harming the plant.

From a distance, all goldenrod appears pretty much alike. However, there are actually 125 species of them that grow in the United States. The Southeast is home to at least 50 species. Botanists often can't agree on how many types of goldenrod exist. One reason for this is that they often hybridize, making identification difficult even for the experts.

If you want to try goldenrod in your garden, you can either purchase cultivated varieties from nurseries that specialize in native plants or take them from the wild.

If you collect plants from the wild, make sure you obtain permission from the landowner on whose land they are growing. Then, look at a number of stands of goldenrod while they are in full bloom. When you find one that has the proper height and flowering characteristics, flag it. Then come back and dig it up the following spring, when you can set it out in your garden.

When I found that some goldenrod had taken root in one of my nectar-feeder gardens last spring, I didn't pull it up. While a bevy of gorgeous blooms was eventually produced, the plants grew to be at least four feet tall—far too tall for the spot they had commandeered. Consequently, I removed the pioneering plants this past spring.

In my yard, goldenrod is now confined to the north boundary of my backyard. Here, they intermingle with a number of other native plants that serve as a twenty-five-foot-wide natural border with my neighbor.

Should you decide to incorporate cultivated varieties into the landscape around your home, begin by taking a visit to a nursery that specializes in native plants. There you can choose varieties based on when they bloom (from mid to late summer to fall), height (one-and-a-half to more than four feet tall), leaf size, texture, and color as well as whether they grow best in wet or dry sites.

If you have never visited a stand of goldenrod in full bloom, you are in for a real treat. When you do, I strongly suggest that you bring a camera and close-focusing binoculars. You will need this equipment to fully appreciate the amazing numbers and varieties of insects you will find there. Some of the gorgeous insects I have discovered on goldenrod plumes are great purple, gray and red-banded hairstreaks and ailanthus webworm moths as well as brightly colored bees, wasps, and hornets.

If you allow goldenrods plants to remain standing throughout the winter, they will provide cover for songbirds, rabbits, and small mammals. The seeds will be eaten by a number of birds and small mammals. The American goldfinch is particularly fond of goldenrod seeds. Among the other birds that dine on the tiny seeds are swamp sparrows, eastern towhees, pine siskins, and dark-eyed juncos. If you live in the mountains, don't be surprised to see ruffed grouse eating goldenrod seeds on cold winter days.

The therapeutic values of goldenrod have been touted for centuries. In fact, the plant's genus name *Solidago* means "to make whole." The first European settlers in North America used goldenrod in steam baths and to brew a tea-like drink. It is said that the tea was used to treat sore throats and as a poultice on wounds and skin ulcers. Today some herbalists use the plant as a diuretic, urinary antiseptic, and anti-inflammatory drug.

If goldenrod doesn't currently grace your yard, next spring set some plants out in a flower bed, in a natural border or an overlooked corner of your yard. When you do, you will be adding another beautiful bit of diversity to your landscape. Then, next fall, enjoy the spectacular prelude to the eye-popping fall-foliage extravaganza without having to leave your yard.

MISTLETOE IS MORE THAN A HOLIDAY DECORATION

N ow that the beautiful autumn foliage blankets the ground, forming a tapestry of gold, orange, red, and brown, one can't help but take notice of green splotches of mistletoe clinging to the now-bare branches of trees across the county. While we do not give much thought to this plant throughout most of the year, we do so at Christmas. It, along with holly, poinsettias, and ever-green trees, is forever linked to this special holiday. That it is also a valuable wildlife food plant should not be overlooked.

Since before recorded time, mistletoe was thought to contain magical powers. In Sweden, sword handles were hewn from mistle-toe in the belief that this special wood would offer protection from witches. Across the globe in Japan, women would eat the plant in hopes of conceiving a child. In Wales, farmers would tie mistletoe to the horns of the first cow that gave birth in the new year, con-vinced this would ensure the prospering of their herds during the rest of the year. African warriors would sometimes carry mistletoe into battle to protect themselves from injury.

Mistletoe is also purported to have therapeutic powers. Over the centuries, this parasitic plant has been used to cure everything from itching to toothaches.

Our custom of adorning our homes with mistletoe quite possibly originated with the druids. The ancient druids would hang mistletoe in their homes during winter in the belief that they were providing warm sanctuaries for woodland spirits that supposedly hid in mistletoe during the winter.

These early people also believed that not everyone could harvest mistletoe. No, indeed. This magical plant could be cut only with a golden sickle wielded by white-robed priests on the sixth day of the new moon.

The custom of kissing beneath a frond of mistletoe probably evolved from Norse mythology. One Nordic myth tells us that because mistletoe was dedicated to the Goddess of Love, if a couple embraces beneath a tree hosting mistletoe, the lovers will be healthy and experience good luck.

Washington Irving, author of *The Legend of Sleepy Hollow,* advised that good manners dictate kissing is allowed under a branch of mistletoe only while berries are still present. Each time a kiss is stolen, the thief is supposed to remove a berry. The rash attempt to kiss another beneath a berryless sprig of mistletoe is out of line.

Although the alleged values of mistletoe to mankind may be more fiction than fact, mistletoe is indeed a great wildlife food plant.

One of our most stunning butterflies, the iridescent blue great purple hairstreak lays its eggs only on mistletoe. Without mistletoe, we would be denied the opportunity to enjoy the sight of this gossamer-winged insect's breathtaking beauty.

Some seventeen species of wildlife eat mistletoe berries. They are favorites of both cedar waxwings and eastern bluebirds. The seemingly translucent white berries are also eaten by American and fish crows and hermit thrushes as well as robins and other birds.

Believe it or not, white-tailed deer never miss a chance to eat mistletoe foliage. However, since whitetails cannot fly like Santa's reindeer, our deer must wait until a clump of mistletoe falls out of a tree or a tree harboring mistletoe topples in order to dine on it.

It is a little known fact that mistletoe played a role in the reintroduction of the white-tailed deer in the state of Georgia. Most of the deer used in restocking efforts in the Peach State were trapped in those few places in the state that still harbored deer. These deer were captured and subsequently released in locales where the large mammals were scarce or nonexistent. The biologists that trapped the deer often baited their large wooden deer traps with mistletoe, knowing that this was a highly successful bait.

I think you would agree that this wildlife food plant's rise from once being banned from Christian churches because of its prominent place in pagan mythology to becoming one of the most recognizable symbols of Christmas is truly remarkable. It seems that the magic of Christmas makes anything possible.

Merry Christmas!

PART 6

The Holidays

February 10, 2010

VALENTINE'S DAY IS FOR THE BIRDS

Everyone is familiar with Valentine's Day. It is a day inexorably linked to love, greeting cards, roses, and chocolate candy. Yet if you were to ask folks standing in line to buy a box of Valentine's Day candy where and when this holiday began, few would know the answer. If you told them that birds may have played a key role in the origins of this holiday dedicated to love, they would probably look at you in disbelief.

Down through the ages, several legends have cropped up that purport to explain the origins of this popular holiday. In truth, we will probably never be able to say with absolute certainty the reason we celebrate Valentine's Day on February 14.

Some of the curmudgeons among us are convinced that Valentine's Day is the brainchild of greeting-card and candy man-ufactures. Supposedly, these barons of commerce have cleverly concocted this holiday to sell more of their products to those that are romantically inclined.

Others suggest that the origin of Valentine's Day traces back to Rome during the reign of Claudius II. At that time, he was having trouble enticing men to sign up for his army. He and his advisors were convinced that this was due primarily to the men's unwillingness to leave their wives and families to fight in the far-flung reaches of the Roman Empire. In an effort to alleviate this perplexing problem, the Roman emperor decreed a ban on all marriages.

A defiant priest named Valentine supposedly defied the order and continued to secretly perform marriage ceremonies. When the emperor learned of the priest's actions, he was so enraged that he ordered the priest be slain. His mandate was carried out, and the defiant religious leader is said to have been murdered on February 14 on or about AD 270.

Another popular version of this tale tells us that Valentine was executed because he tried to assist Christians trying to escape Roman prisons. Yet another twist on this story purports that while Valentine was awaiting his execution, he sent a farewell letter to his beloved. The object of his affection just happened to be the jailer's daughter. He supposedly signed the letter "from your Valentine."

Perhaps I am biased, but I prefer to believe that the origins of Valentine's Day stem from a medieval holiday known as the Birds' Wedding Day. It is said that for some unknown reason, folks living in France and England decided that birds begin their breeding season during the middle of February. They even went so far as to designate February 14 as *the* day that their mating actually begins. This day just happened to coincide with a feast day of the early Roman martyr named Valentinus.

Later, as part of the celebration, villagers in the area of Sussex, England, began celebrating the Birds' Wedding Day in an unusual way. Each February 14, before the sun rose above the eastern horizon, young people would set out on a quest to net three birds—two sparrows and an owl. It was considered a good omen if they succeeded, and those that captured the birds were rewarded with gifts.

For the life of me, I don't understand how anybody could come up with February 14 as the day that signaled the beginning of the birds' breeding season. While I don't claim to be an expert on European birds, I suspect that most birds nesting in that part of the world actually begin their mating rituals much later in the year.

Locally, by February 14, the breeding season has begun for only a handful of birds. Bald eagles have been nesting since December. Great horned owls commonly nest in January. The tiny brown-headed nuthatch is already looking for suitable nesting sites and caulking the cracks between the boards of their nest boxes with bits of plant matter like pine needles. Although turkeys won't be breeding for weeks, I have already heard some impatient gobblers gobbling.

I must admit that I am guilty of trying to make sense out of a legend. That is always risky business, because legends rarely, if ever, stand up to scientific scrutiny.

What is important is that this holiday, tucked away in the middle of one of the harshest months of the year, is all about expressing our love for others. As such, on Valentine's Day, let your loved ones know how much they mean to you. Your cards and gifts will turn what will likely be a gloomy winter day into a day to remember. And don't forget to do something special for the birds living in your backyard. Who knows, some of their ancestors may have helped give us Valentine's Day.

Happy Valentine's Day!

HALLOWEEN IS TOUGH ON BATS

O ut of all the animals we associate with Halloween, none has a worse reputation than the bat. This is definitely one of the critters most folks in Monroe County love to hate. However, on Halloween, our ill toward the bat seems to rise to the surface like a bubble in a witch's brew simmering in a large, black cauldron.

For thousands of years, bats have been undeservedly blamed for any number of humankind's problems. Ironically, though, in some cultures the bat is not considered to be a vile creature to be avoided at any cost. Let's take a quick look at some of the folklore swirling around this flying mammal.

In the Ozarks, folks once blamed even the scourge of bedbugs on bats. According to this fanciful tale, daddy longlegs lay their eggs on bats. When these eggs hatch, for reasons that are not explained, bedbugs emerge. Those believing this myth say that proof of this miraculous process is easy to find—all you have to do is crush a daddy longlegs. The scent released by this unfortunate creature smells just like a bedbug. I for one don't quite follow this line of reasoning. Do you?

For some reason, bats are associated with witches. Nobody knows how this came about; however, this belief is shared by members of many cultures. People living on the Isle of Man, for example, once believed that at night, witches would take the form of bats and fly about the countryside on their mischievous missions.

In Scotland, according to one folktale, you can always tell when the witches' hour has arrived. At this time, bats will soar upward from their daytime roosts and then plummet down toward the earth.

In other parts of the world, the flight of the bat has other meanings. In Finland, people once believed that some bats are actually the souls of the dead and that if a bat flies toward you, this is a sure sign that it is actually the soul of a dead family member. Another Finnish legend asserts that while we sleep, our souls often take the shape of a bat. People have long believed that seeing a bat is an omen.

On this side of the Atlantic, the sight of a bat flying low to the ground was once thought to be a sure sign that a storm was on the way. Another tale says that if a bat is spotted flying around a house three times, somebody will soon die.

Another fable alleges that a bat flying into a house is an omen that disasters will soon befall the unfortunate people who live there. This folktale makes little sense when you consider that throughout much of human history, people lived in domiciles that lacked windows. As such, they often shared their homes with bats and any number of other flying critters.

Bats are also associated with good luck. In the Orient, for example, bats are deemed symbols of prosperity and happiness. In Germany, many once held the belief that the heart of a bat would protect them from evil spirits. A spinoff of this is a legend that dates back to the Middle Ages. Supposedly, this tale promises that if you tie a bat's heart to your sleeve, you will be dealt good cards.

In Europe, gypsies often hung small bags of dried bat parts around the necks of their children as good-luck charms.

Some people have actually looked to bats in affairs of the heart. A powerful love potion was supposedly created by burning incense over the body of a bat buried at a crossroads. Another fable advises young women to shake a few drops of bat blood into a beer being consumed by their beloved. When he drinks the resulting concoction, it will cause the young man to look upon her in a loving way.

Ironically, while in this day and time few people believe in the fanciful myths associated with this creature, many people still don't think kindly of bats. In truth, the bat is actually an important wildlife neighbor deserving of our admiration and not scorn. In fact, when you learn more about bats, you quickly realize that their life histories and adaptations are far more remarkable than the myths that have forever sullied their reputation.

THE ORIGIN OF THANKSGIVING

For most of us, wildlife and hunting are no longer part of the fabric of Thanksgiving. However, things were quite different 380 years ago when the pilgrims celebrated their first Thanksgiving at Plymouth Colony.

Since we attended elementary school, we have been taught that turkey was the main dish served at the first Thanksgiving. Who can forget having to color pictures of turkeys in elementary school prior to the Thanksgiving holiday? Indeed, turkey was served at the first Thanksgiving celebrated in Plymouth Colony in 1621. However, it was far from the main dish enjoyed by the pilgrims at this festive occasion.

The first Thanksgiving was observed less than a year after the pilgrims arrived at what is now known as Plymouth. The first winter in the New World was harsh on the colonists, and before the end of their first year, their numbers had been cut roughly in half. The number of colonists who died in this short span of time would have been even greater had they not discovered corn stored under piles of rocks by the Native Americans living in the area.

During the spring following their arrival, the pilgrims planted about twenty acres of Indian corn and six acres of barley and peas. While the corn crop did well, the barley crop could at best be rated fair. The pea crop, on the other hand, was a dismal failure.

After the colonists gathered their crops, they decided to celebrate the fruits of their labors by holding a Thanksgiving festival lasting several days.

The governor sent out a number of groups to collect whatever wild foods they could find. At this time, Plymouth harbor was literally alive with fish and shellfish. Ducks and geese were also abundant. In addition, the surrounding countryside teemed with turkeys, deer, grouse, and other wild game. The colony's fishermen and hunters had little trouble bringing home a bounty of wild foods for the celebration. One hunting party, for example, shot enough ducks and geese in a single day to supply more than 150 colonists with enough food for a week.

When all the food was assembled, it was a sight to behold. Chickens were augmented by oysters, eels, herring, bass, geese, and ducks. The menu also included stewed pumpkins, corn, and other vegetables as well as pudding, soups, deer, and turkey. Some of the written accounts of the event indicate that turkey was not the main course and was served only later in the festivities.

A couple of days into the first Thanksgiving, Chief Massasoit and some ninety of his Wampanoag warriors joined the celebration. After a few days, it became evident that the Native Americans had every intention of staying longer than the pilgrims had anticipated. Fearing they would exhaust their winter food supply, they requested that Chief Massasoit send some of his warriors out to harvest more game. The chief agreed to this call for help, and very quickly his men returned with five deer.

Throughout the first Thanksgiving, the pilgrims sang and danced. One of the most popular songs heard during the holiday was the Psalm 23. Dancing included contests to see who could jig the longest. The children engaged in shouting contests, pillow-pushing bouts, and tugs of war. Captain Miles Standish led his men in shooting matches. They also competed in log tossing and contests to see if they could knock one another off logs.

Indeed, things have changed dramatically over the centuries. For example, Thanksgiving has been reduced to a single day. Few Monroe County hunters take to the woods on a traditional Thanksgiving Day hunt. Fewer still will sing and dance.

As for food, although pumpkin and turkey will share top billing on many of our tables, fish, deer, and ducks will be served in a few homes. Regardless of what we eat this Thanksgiving, let's not forget to give thanks for the bounty of food on our table and the wonderful country in which we live. In spite of all that we have gone through during the past few months, we Americans have every reason to be as thankful for our blessings as were the pilgrims in 1621.

DOGS AND THE THANKSGIVING TURKEY

I t is difficult to think of Thanksgiving dinner without picturing a large roasted turkey sitting on a platter in the center of a dining room table surrounded with more food than you and your family could ever possibly eat. More than likely, the mouthwatering turkey was purchased at your local grocery store. However, if there is a turkey hunter in the house, it might have been harvested in a sun-dappled hardwood draw last spring. In days long past, the turkey served at the festive holiday might have found its way to the table with the help of a dog.

That's right. I said a dog. Now, I'm not talking about the family pet, whose only connection with a turkey is gobbling (no pun intended) up those leftover scraps placed in its food bowl after the family has enjoyed a scrumptious Thanksgiving dinner. These dogs were dogs trained to hunt turkeys.

Most Native American tribes ate wild turkey. They killed these birds in a number of ways, ranging from shooting them with darts, arrows, and spears to trapping. In some cases, they even used dogs to hunt turkeys. One journal entry written in Jamestown in 1608 noted that Native Americans kept cur dogs that were used for hunting turkeys and other game.

Native Americans taught the colonists how to hunt turkeys. The newcomers quickly learned that most of the turkey-hunting techniques used by the native hunters took considerable skill and patience. As might be expected, many colonial hunters opted to hunt turkeys the easiest way—with dogs.

Soon, turkeys were pursued with dogs for sport as well as for food. In Louisiana, for example, turkey hunting with dogs was popular as early as 1724.

As settlers moved westward, they brought with them the sport of hunting turkeys with dogs. In these wide-open spaces, greyhounds were the dogs of choice. Teddy Roosevelt in a book published in 1885 entitled *Hunting Trips of a Ranchman* wrote about Californian and Texas horsemen using greyhounds to hunt a variety of game, including antelope, rabbit, and wild turkey.

During the early 1900s, using dogs to hunt turkeys was both legal and a popular way to hunt the large birds in Alabama and a number of other states. In fact, throughout the South, hunting turkeys with dogs in the fall was considered a tradition.

In the 1950s, Leigh Perkins of the Orvis Corporation, noted for its fly-fishing gear, wrote of a fall turkey hunt in Georgia during which they used turkey dogs to both flush the birds off the roost and retrieve those that were wounded. Perkins wrote that his Brittany was able to locate "winged" birds that had traveled two miles.

The use of dogs to locate wounded turkeys was popular throughout much of the nineteenth and early twentieth centuries. In fact, John James Audubon in an 1840 journal entry recorded that hunters used dogs to locate turkeys that would never have been found by hunters without their aid.

Although the ability to find a wounded bird was considered a plus, what early turkey hunters prized most of all were dogs that could silently trail a flock of turkeys. These dogs were taught not to bark until they flushed the flock. Turkey dogs were also trained not to bark while a hunter attempted to call the scattered birds close enough for a shot.

As you might imagine, not all dogs make good turkey dogs. While a number of breeds have been used for this task, more often than not, the best proved to be pointers and setters.

In recent years, hunting turkeys with dogs has enjoyed a revival. There is even an American Wild Turkey Hunting Dog Association.

Out of the forty-four states that permit fall turkey hunting, thirty allow hunters to use dogs. Four states—Nebraska, Utah, Montana, and Tennessee—even allow hunters to use dogs during the spring hunting season. Fall turkey hunting and using dogs to hunt turkeys, however, is illegal in Georgia.

As such, it is unlikely that hunting a Thanksgiving turkey with a turkey dog will become a tradition here any time soon. That's fine with me. I enjoy trying to outwit a turkey on a dazzling spring morning all by myself. If I'm not successful in bagging a long-bearded gobbler, I know I can always find a turkey in my local grocery store—and I don't need a dog to do it.

Happy Thanksgiving!

THANKSGIVING TURKEYS FROM MERRY OLD ENGLAND?

N o, this isn't the recall notice of a food product imported from a foreign county. In a strange twist of fate, the forty-five million turkeys consumed by Americans this Thanksgiving are direct descendants of domestic turkeys imported in Europe centuries ago.

It seems that long before the pilgrims set foot on Plymouth Rock, turkeys from the Americas had already made their way to Europe. Even though wild turkeys aren't native to England or anywhere else in the Old World, the early European colonists were familiar with this large, long-legged bird. In fact, an early journalist recorded in his diary that the turkeys found here were smaller and lighter in color than those in Europe.

Spanish explorers returning from an expedition to what is now known as Mexico in 1518 have long been credited with bringing turkeys to Spain. Twenty-three years later, domestic turkeys were being raised in England.

The legs were knocked out from under this theory when it came to light that what appear to be turkeys are depicted in a mural and frieze adorning a German cathedral built in the 1200s. The artist who created the frieze was a member of a league that engaged in trade with Norse sailors that regularly made trips to Greenland. This opens up the possibility that Norsemen brought wild turkeys with them on voyages to Greenland or North America long before the Spanish set foot in the New World.

Early American colonists didn't domesticate turkeys. The turkeys served at their tables were birds taken from the wild. Later, domesticated turkeys shipped to America from Europe formed the nucleus of the domestic flocks raised here ever since.

A few Indian tribes living in Mexico and what is now the United States did, however, succeed in domesticating native wild turkeys. The only Native Americans living in eastern North America known to have domesticated turkeys made their home in portions of Virginia and North Carolina. In the Southwest, the Pueblos actually kept turkeys in their cliff dwellings.

When Cortez encountered the Aztecs in 1517, he found that the raptors in Emperor Montezuma's vast collection of birds of prey were fed five hundred domestic turkeys a day.

Native Americans used turkeys for a number of purposes other than food. Turkey bones were fashioned into beads, projectile points, awls, and spoons. Turkey feathers were used to create artwork. They were even woven into fabrics. Wing feathers were crafted into arrow fletching.

While most of us savor the taste of roast turkey, some early settlers found the meat of certain turkeys to be nauseous. Since the turkey vulture looks somewhat like a turkey, do you suppose they tried to eat these scavengers, thinking they were turkeys?

In Virginia, Native Americans became concerned when they found that settlers were actually making soup from boiled venison and turkey. They feared this unholy union would offend their spirits and cause wild game to abandon the woodlands in the area.

Today, our domestic turkey is a far different critter than the wary wild turkeys that inhabit our fields and forests. They are primarily represented by four breeds—the bronze, Narragansett, white Holland, and bourbon red. Some have been bred to have such large chests and thighs that they sometimes tip the scales at more than fifty pounds. Many are so large they can't even fly short distances and often fall over when they try to run. Their colors range from bronze and black to white. While today's domestic breeds only superficially look like wild turkeys, they are low in fat and cholesterol and are tastier than their ancestors. This, coupled with the fact that wild turkey populations are surging upward in the Peach State and elsewhere across the country, has made the turkey more popular than it has ever been. Indeed, the turkey has come a long way in the past four hundred years.

I think you will agree that the turkey took a roundabout route to reach our dining-room tables at Thanksgiving. I for one am glad it didn't get lost along the way.

November 24, 2010

THANKSGIVING DINNER
IS NOT WHAT IT USED TO BE

When you and your family sit down to Thanksgiving dinner, the meal you will all enjoy is going to be far different than that served at the first Thanksgiving celebrated in 1621.

As important as this celebration was to the pilgrims, it is surprising that the journals written at the time don't provide us with many details regarding what was actually served. In fact, the only foods mentioned by name were venison and birds. However, since historians know what foods were commonly eaten at that time, we have a pretty good idea what the Pilgrims and their Native American guests probably ate at the first Thanksgiving. With that in mind, let's compare the first Thanksgiving with how we celebrate it today.

It is believed that fifty-three pilgrims and ninety Wampanoag Indians attended the first Thanksgiving. The celebration lasted three whole days in mid-October. Today, the holiday is observed on a single day—the fourth Thursday in November.

Can you imagine what it would be like trying to eat Thanksgiving dinner without a fork? Probably not. However, since forks were not used in Great Britain until the eighteenth century, forks were not on the table at the first Thanksgiving.

Providing enough food for those assembled proved to be quite a chore. Since the colonists didn't have a lot of food to spare, it is said that the Wampanoags actually provided much of the food eaten during the holiday. In preparation for the grand event, the pilgrims' leader, William Bradford, sent out hunting and fishing parties to harvest a bounty of wild foods. In fact, without wild game and fish, the pilgrims would have had meager pickings during their three-day feast. It was said that hunters brought back enough birds to feed the crowd for an entire week. Fearing that the revelers would run out of food after the first day of the celebration, Chief Massasoit dispatched some of his warriors to shoot more game. They returned with five deer.

It is interesting to note that at the event, Native American men and women ate together. In comparison, pilgrim women stood behind the menfolk while they ate. Only when they finished were the women permitted to sit down and eat.

Although some Monroe Countians prefer to eat ham on Thanksgiving, by far the meat most often eaten on this holiday is turkey. You might be surprised to learn, therefore, that turkey was not the main course at the first Thanksgiving. In fact, some suggest they were not eaten at all during the 1621 celebrations. Other historians share the opinion that wild turkeys were not put on the table until the festivities were well underway. If they were served, they were more than likely boiled or roasted.

Along with turkey, other meats served were venison, roasted wild ducks, geese, and ruffed grouse. Fish and shellfish were in abundance along the shoreline. Consequently, the meal more than likely included seethed (boiled) lobster, cod, and other saltwater delicacies. One of the favorite ways to cook fish was to wrap them in leaves and roast them on a bed of hot coals.

Nowadays, both white and sweet potatoes are among our Thanksgiving favorites. However, since they were unknown in that part of the world in 1621, they were absent from the pilgrim's menu.

One of your favorite Thanksgiving dishes is probably stuffing. It too was missing from the table.

Cranberries are also inexorably linked to Thanksgiving dinner. In spite of the fact that tons of these tangy berries are raised in Massachusetts annually, they were not grown in and around Plymouth at that time.

One berry that was undoubtedly eaten at the first Thanksgiving was the whortleberry. Right about now, you are probably asking yourself, "What in the world is a whortleberry?"

Whortleberry is simply another name for the blueberry. Whortleberries were dried and served in a number of dishes, including a pudding made with corn. It would be safe to say that few of us will be dining on whortleberry and corn pudding this year.

Squash is another popular Thanksgiving dish. Both butternut and winter squash grace our plates today. Squash was probably also served at the first Thanksgiving.

Other vegetables that made their way to the table were corn and peas. Since food preservation was a problem, no fresh corn or pea dishes were served. Corn was ground into cornmeal and served as a major ingredient in a number of dishes. Peas were served much as they are today.

Pumpkin pie is also a Thanksgiving favorite. In fact, I would venture to say that more pumpkin pie is eaten at Thanksgiving than at any other time of the year. While pumpkins were likely on the menu, the pilgrims didn't serve them in a pie. Pumpkins were simply dropped into the coals of a hot fire and roasted.

Speaking of pies, what would Thanksgiving be like without pecan pie? Pecan pie is another item that didn't make it to the table at the first Thanksgiving. First of all, the colonists would not have had access to any pecans. Additionally, although they brought sugar with them from England, more than likely it was used up by the time the first Thanksgiving was celebrated. As cooks know, you can't make pecan pie without lots of sugar.

Yes, the way we celebrate Thanksgiving and eat Thanksgiving dinner has really changed over the centuries. However, one thing hasn't been altered. Like the pilgrims, on this special holiday, we always give thanks for all of our blessings.

I hope you and yours will have happy Thanksgiving!

A CHRISTMAS TREE BEDECKED WITH BUTTERFLIES

O ver the centuries, many legends have become woven into the fabric of Christmas. Some of the most popular of these fables are associated with animals. These stories typically involve birds and mammals that allegedly witnessed the birth of Christ. However, at least one legend concerns butterflies and tells a tale that took place much later.

The story tells us that many years ago on Christmas Eve, a little girl sat beside the Christmas tree that stood in the corner of her small home. The tree had been cut from the nearby woods earlier in the day. Since her family was very poor, the green branches of the tree held no colorful Christmas ornaments. However, a small paper star had been placed atop the tree to represent the star that led the Three Wise Men to the manger where Christ was born.

The youngster went to sleep wishing that she and her family had been able to better decorate their beautiful tree. As we all know, marvelous events are purported to take place on Christmas Eve. Such was the case in this humble home. When the girl awoke the next morning, the tree was covered with scores of beautiful butterflies whose bodies were made of crystal and their wings of gold. It seems that the tree had been festooned with tiny chrysalises. During the night, warmed by the heat of the fire, the jewel-like butterflies had emerged from their fragile chrysalises to bedazzle the little girl and her family with the most stunning Christmas tree they had ever seen.

Decorating Christmas trees with butterfly ornaments is growing in popularity. In fact, some folks use butterfly ornaments exclusively on their Christmas trees. However, as gorgeous as these ornaments are, none can match the breathtaking beauty of the live butterflies they are designed to represent.

With this in mind, I asked myself if it would be possible to bedeck a Christmas tree with live butterflies native to Monroe County, which would I select? Here is what I came up with.

I would begin by placing an adult monarch butterfly on my tree. This familiar butterfly's wings have black borders. Embedded in the borders are white spots. The background color of the wings is orange.

I would also hang a number of Monarch chrysalises on the tree. They are light green in color and adorned with tiny gold dots. They remind me of the precious gifts bestowed on the Christ child by the Three Wise Men.

I would be remiss if I didn't scatter a number of cloudless sulphurs on the feathery branches of the tree. These bright-yellow butterflies would imitate the light provided by candles years ago.

The great purple hairstreak would have a place on my tree. While this butterfly is not actually purple, the upper sides of its wings are royal blue. In addition, its host plant is mistletoe, a plant that is traditionally displayed in our homes at Christmas.

I would also find a place for the red-banded hairstreak. This demure butterfly is a flying jewel. Its underwings are highlighted with distinctive red-orange bands. The inclusion of this butterfly is a reminder that wonderful gifts often come in small packages.

The gulf fritillary also deserves a spot on my tree. The upper sides of its wings are bright orange. The bottoms are festooned with silver spots reminiscent of the shiny tinsel that is often draped on Christmas trees.

Another reason the gulf fritillary deserves inclusion on my tree is because its host plant is the passion flower. Early Spanish explorers marveled at the complex, beautiful flower produced by this lowly vine. To them, the flower depicts the crucifixion of Christ.

I would include the common buckeye on my tree simply because, while it is one of our most common butterflies, it is also one of the most beautiful butterflies found in the county. In addition, the large blue, black, and orange spots trimmed in yellow and black resemble tiny Christmas ornaments.

I would add the red admiral to my list of butterfly ornaments because the butterfly's upper wings are highlighted with red, white, and blue. The prominent reddish-to-orange bands look much like the brightly colored ribbons used to wrap Christmas presents.

Our state butterfly, the eastern tiger swallowtail, is one of our most gorgeous and easily identifiable butterflies. Its bright-yellow wings are highlighted with tigerlike stripes. Poised against the dark-green needles of a Christmas tree, this butterfly would make a stunning ornament.

The falcate orangetip is a small butterfly seen only during the spring. This tiny beauty has snow-white wings tipped with orange. How can you have a Christmas tree without a few predominantly white decorations?

Last but not least, I would find a place for the juniper hairstreak. While the bright olive-green butterfly is not the most beautiful butterfly found in our county, it deserves to be included because it spends most of its life on or near its host plant, the Christmas tree of the South—the red cedar.

Well, there you have it. While I will never actually see a tree bedecked in these beautiful ornaments in real life, I can close my eyes and see one standing in the corner of my living room. I wish that you could see it too!

Merry Christmas.

THE POINSETTIA

The poinsettia is one of the most beautiful plants that is forever linked with Christmas. Like the other plants we associate with this special holiday, a number of legends and myths swirl around this symbol of the holiday season.

One popular legend tells us that poinsettias became associated to Christmas because of an event that took place many years ago on Christmas Eve in Mexico. It seems that on this most holy night, local townspeople were making their annual pilgrimage to their cathedral, bearing gifts for Jesus. All of the people making the trek were filled with hope and joy—except for one poor little girl.

When she reached the heavy wooden doors of the church, she stopped, fell to her knees, and began to pray to the Christ Child. Her simple, heartfelt prayer expressed her disappointment at being unable to place a gift on the cathedral's altar.

As she finished her prayer and wiped her tear-filled eyes, her gaze focused on a small clearing located near the church. As she stared blankly at the clearing, she noticed a telltale movement. Moving closer, she found that a small plant was miraculously springing from the hard earth. As she stood transfixed, the mysterious plant steadily grew until it was about four feet tall. Then, as soon as it stopped growing, vibrant red blooms suddenly appeared.

As the young girl gazed in wonder at the miracle she alone had witnessed, it occurred to her that the red flowers would make a perfect gift for Jesus. She quickly picked a bouquet of these special flowers and lovingly placed them on the altar among the gifts left behind by the other worshipers.

As time went on, the mysterious plants blanketed the entire clearing and eventually spread throughout the city. Before long, the remarkable red-flowered plants could be found throughout Mexico.

This marvelous plant was named in honor of Joel Poinsett. Poinsett served as the US minster to Mexico from 1829 to 1833. This inveterate world traveler collected plants wherever he went. During his service in Mexico, he became captivated by plants that turned red during the Christmas season. Locally, the name of the plant that blooms during this special time of the year translates as "the flower of the blessed night" in honor of the miracle witnessed by a poor little peasant girl so many years before.

His careful study of the plant revealed that what was thought to be a red flower was not a flower at all. What was mistaken for flower petals were actually specialized leaves called bracts. The plant's blossoms were instead quite small, yellow, and inconspicuous.

Poinsett's fascination with the flower of the blessed night led to his sending a number of the plants back to his South Carolina plantation. Eventually, cuttings made from these plants were sent to a number of American plant enthusiasts.

A few years after his return to the United States, botanists renamed the flower of the blessed bight the poinsettia in his honor.

Eventually, horticulturalists learned that poinsettias could be encouraged to bloom at Christmas anywhere in the world by regulating the amount of light to which the plant is exposed. This is actually a very simple process. In October, simply place your poinsettias in a dark place, such as a closet, for fourteen hours per day. During the daylight hours, expose the plants to no more than ten hours of sunlight. If you continue this process for ten weeks, your poinsettias will reward you with red blossoms at Christmas.

In Mexico, poinsettias soar to a height of ten feet and bear red, white, or pink bracts. While poinsettias can be used as garden plants from extreme south Georgia into Florida, locally they are killed by the frost. However, I have seen some poinsettias that are planted adjacent to the foundations of homes exist for years. These plants, however, display only traces of red.

Surveys have shown that the majority of Americans believe the poinsettia to be poisonous. It is thought this belief stems from an erroneous report circulated in 1919 that stated a two-year-old child of an army officer died after eating poinsettia leaves. In truth, the prestigious American Medical Association in its *Handbook of Poisonous and Injurious Plants* states that eating poinsettia leaves causes nothing more severe than occasional vomiting. Researchers have found that a child tipping the scales at fifty pounds would have to eat some one and a quarter pounds of poinsettia leaves (approximately five hundred to six hundred leaves) to pose a possible serious health threat.

With this in mind, enjoy the crimson glory of the poinsettia this holiday season, keeping in mind the message of the Mexican legend of a little girl and her special Christmas gift.

October 27, 2010

OWLS, FOLKLORE, AND HALLOWEEN

The owl is one of a handful of animals seemingly forever linked to Halloween. This is unfortunate, because it is totally undeserving of being associated with superstition, witches, and things that go bump in the night.

Long before there ever was a Halloween, many people throughout the world associated the owl with death, misfortune, and even witches. The reasons for this have been lost in the mists of time. Some suggest this was perhaps linked to the bird's ability to see extremely well at night, a time when without the aid of a light, we mortals stumble about blindly.

For thousands of years, mankind has tried to find an explanation for the bird's amazing nighttime vision. To many, there was only one answer—witches must have cast a magical spell on these denizens of the night, enabling them to fly about as easily as a sparrow or hawk does in the daylight.

The belief that owls consorted with witches and other unsavory characters has long been widespread in many countries. This is reflected in the fact that in many societies, the word for *owl* and *witch* is the same.

When you gaze at an owl, you immediately notice that unlike most birds, its head is oval or round, and its large eyes face forward. In fact, the owl's face is so humanlike that in parts of the world, people were convinced that owls were actually humans whom witches had magically transformed into owls.

The thing that seems to unnerve people most is not the bird's appearance but its call. Throughout time, the call of an owl has been considered a harbinger of bad tidings.

To the Chinese, the owl's call has long been interpreted as a sign that misfortune would soon befall anyone unlucky enough to hear it. The Hindus shared similar misgivings. It was said that the call of an owl meant that somebody would soon die or suffer harm. One of the worst things that could befall a Hindu village was for an owl to alight atop a hut. When this happened, villagers believed the only way they could avoid a calamity was to kill the owl, burn its body, and scatter its ashes into a river. Additionally, nobody was allowed back into that hut until the thatch touched by the owl was torn out and replaced.

The Romans were convinced that owls were messengers of death. Whenever they heard an owl's call, they too made every effort to slay and burn it and scatter its ashes onto the surface of a river.

Christopher Columbus also harbored contempt for owls. While preparing for one of his voyages across the Atlantic, he penned in his journal that owls were "funeral birds of night."

In Britain, the barn owl was dubbed the death owl. Consequently, it is not surprising that Shakespeare incorporated owl calls into many of his masterpieces to foretell death or create foreboding overtones.

Remarkably, even Native American tribes shared superstitions regarding owls. Many tribes thought that owls possessed great mystical powers. They also believed that the spirits used owls to warn of impeding death.

The Pima Indians of the Southwest practiced the custom of placing owl feathers into the hand of someone thought to be on the verge of passing on. By so doing, they believed an owl would spot the feathers and realize that the one clasping them was prepared to take the journey to the afterlife.

Closer to home, great horned, barred, and screech owls played important roles in the spiritual life of the Cherokees. They believed that these owls, all of which are permanent residents in Monroe County, could communicate with their shamans in a strange, silent tongue. The great horned owl, which they called the Magic Maker, was considered to be the most important of the three. However, each was supposedly imbued with the power to bring illness upon anyone who veered from the straight and narrow.

The folklore of early European settlers is rich with fanciful tales about owls. One folktale tells us that the sound of a screech owl's call outside one's home was a sure sign of impending death or illness. The tale went on to say that if an owl's call was heard outside the home of somebody that was ill, the only way to prevent this person from dying was to dispatch the bird and place its carcass on his or her chest.

This fear of owls was so pervasive that parents taught their children that under no circumstances should they ever imitate a screech owl. They believed that if a screech owl heard such a call coming from a cabin, it would begin hanging around and eventually fly down the chimney. Once inside, it would scatter hot coals about the floor, which in turn would burn the home to the ground.

Today, most folks don't place much stock in such strange superstitions. However, in this age of enlightenment, this bird—often called Mother Nature's mouse trap—remains regrettably and indelibly linked to Halloween.

PART 7

Food, Water, Nest Boxes, and More

THE BASICS OF WINTER BIRD FEEDING

Would you believe that you can attract the greatest variety of birds to your backyard feeding station for the least cost by using only three or four different kinds of feeders and foods? It's true.

During the winter, you will attract the most birds by offering them seeds. However, like us, birds prefer some foods over others. The two seeds that are relished far and away more than any others are black oil sunflower seeds and white proso millet.

The problem is that most of us buy mixed seed that contains a wide variety of seeds, such as cracked corn, wheat, milo, and others. Although these mixes usually contain some white proso millet and black oil sunflower seeds, they are also composed of large quantities of seeds that are way down on the birds' list of preferred food. Consequently, when you buy an inexpensive wild birdseed mix, much of the seed goes uneaten and eventually becomes contaminated with bacteria and fungi that can actually kill the birds you are trying to feed.

If you don't believe it, fill your feeder with an inexpensive bird-seed mixture. After a week or so, you will undoubtedly find literally hundreds of round, reddish brown seeds piled up below your feeder. These are milo seeds. Locally, our feeder birds would rather toss them out of the feeding tray than eat them. Consequently, while you paid a little less for the mix, the wasted seed quickly offsets what appeared to be a great bargain.

There are some very good wild birdseed mixes that will cost a little more. All of these have high percentages of white proso millet and black oil sunflower seeds. However, the little bit extra you pay for the mixture will make a huge difference in controlling waste seed and disease.

Ideally, the best solution to this problem is to buy black oil sunflower seeds and white proso millet in bulk and either feed them separately or in a mixture that you create yourself.

The lengthy list of birds that will dine on seeds in the winter at your feeder includes sparrows (field, chipping, white-throated), eastern towhees, Carolina chickadees, dark-eyed juncos, tufted titmice, red-winged blackbirds, house and purple finches, mourning doves, blue jays, and Eurasian collared-doves, northern cardinals, brown-headed nuthatches, American goldfinches, and pine siskins, to name a few.

Should you want to expand your guest list, add suet to your menu. From my experience, the best suet is one that contains peanuts and/or peanut butter. The birds that will dine on suet include the Carolina wren, downy and hairy woodpeckers, brown thrasher, and ruby-crowned kinglet as well as orange-crowned and pine warblers. All of these birds are predominantly insect eaters.

Suet is best offered in an inexpensive, rectangular wire cage. Although birds will visit suet feeders that dangle in the breeze, they seem to prefer to eat at feeders attached to a stationary object, such as a tree or post.

If you watch birds for very long, you quickly learn that certain birds prefer to feed on or near the ground while others seem to like to eat at an elevated feeder. For example, white-throated sparrows, eastern towhees, and mourning doves like to dine on the ground. Meanwhile, chickadees, titmice, and woodpeckers would rather feed in a lofty feeder. Consequently, scattering some seed on the ground as well as providing feeders located above the ground will help attract more birds.

The types of feeders I would recommend are a feeding table, tube, and hopper feeders. Bird-feeding tables are simply flat boards on which seed is scattered. The best feeding tables are equipped with quarter-inch holes to drain away excess water. Some of these feeders even come equipped with a roof that helps keep the seed dry.

Bird tables can easily be constructed out of scraps of lumber. Tables can be placed directly on the ground, but by adding four short legs, you can elevate the table slightly above the ground. Some designs even allow you to mount them atop poles or posts.

Feeding tubes and hoppers are perhaps the most popular seed feeders. Food is poured into them and is dispensed at small feeding trays or portals. One advantage of using a large hopper or tube feeder is that it doesn't require refilling every day.

Once birds are enticed to regularly visit a winter feeding station, you can expand both the number and types of feeders and menu items. If you do, you will quickly learn that although the numbers of different kinds of wintering birds using your feeders will not appreciably change, the total numbers of birds feeding in your yard often will increase. However, it is always fun to see what unusual food offerings the birds will use. In the meantime, sit back, pour yourself a cup of coffee, and enjoy the parade of birds feeding just outside your window.

November 7, 2002

PEANUT BUTTER—KIDS AND BIRDS LOVE IT!

If there is one thing that kids and birds have in common, it is their love for peanut butter. That's right—as strange as it seems, the oily, soft spread that we love to smear on crackers or combine with jelly to create a mouthwatering sandwich is also a favorite with a host of birds.

We will never know who first came up with the ingenious idea of feeding peanut butter to birds. I have often wondered whatever possessed somebody to think that peanut butter might be something birds would even stick their bills into. It sure doesn't look like anything that Mother Nature ever put on her natural banquet table. No matter—what is important is the fact that birds can't seem to get enough of it, especially during the winter.

While some folks are very picky about the brand of peanut butter they eat or whether it is chunky or creamy, our bird neighbors don't seem to care. Consequently, when I buy peanut butter for the birds I host in my backyard, I stay away from Peter Pan, Jiff, and other name brands and buy the cheapest brand I can find. In addition, I have found that the birds don't mind whether I offer them chucky or creamy-style peanut butter.

Peanut butter can be fed to birds in a variety of ways. Some folks simply spread it on pine cones or on the trunks of trees that have bark with deep crevices. While both methods work fine, most people put it out in homemade feeders.

One of the easiest ways to make a peanut-butter feeder is to cut a one- to one-and-a-half-foot section from a limb measuring two or more inches in diameter. Select a section that has several small branches protruding at odd angles. Cut these smaller branches off, leaving a stub no more than two to three inches long. Above each of these branches, drill a hole a half inch to a full inch deep. Attach a screw ring to the top of the branch, and then tie a piece of cord or wire to the ring. Once you have filled the holes with peanut butter and hung the feeder near your seed feeders, you are in business.

Another simple feeder can be made by attaching soft-drink bottle caps to a rough-hewn board or limb. A feeder can also be made by attaching a tuna-fish can to a board or post.

Birds will eat peanut butter throughout the year. However, during the summer, it tends to melt and become moldy.

Decades ago, it was reported that birds that eat peanut butter are in danger of having their nasal passageways clogged or choking to death. Since that time, researchers at the prestigious Cornell Lab of Ornithology and elsewhere have not been able to document the death of a single bird that died as a result of eating peanut butter. Personally, during my career as a wildlife biologist, I have never seen or received a report of a bird that died of eating this nutritious spread.

If you are still a little timid about feeding birds peanut butter, you can mix it with corn meal to make the concoction less sticky.

Over the years, homeowners have tried to make their peanut butter offerings even better. These experiments have involved mixing peanut butter with cheese, raisins, birdseed, crushed dog biscuits, and a variety of other items. While all of these additives are eaten by birds, I doubt they make the peanut butter any more desirable.

More than a dozen birds will routinely eat peanut butter in my Monroe County backyard. One of my favorites is the pine warbler. This permanent resident goes unnoticed by most Monroe County homeowners as it spends most of it days foraging for small insects in the tops of pine trees. Pine warbler males have slender bills, two bars on each wing, and bright-yellow breasts and throats; females are duller. Once these bright little sprites become accustomed to your peanut-butter feeder, they will often allow you to approach them to within a few feet.

Carolina chickadees are some of the most frequent visitors to peanut-butter feeders. Their cheery *chick-a-dee-dee-dee* call often lets you know they are close at hand long before they drop down to snatch a bill full of peanut butter.

The list of other potential visitors to peanut-butter feeders includes the brown thrasher, eastern bluebird, red-headed woodpecker, red-bellied woodpecker, yellow-rumped warbler, tufted titmouse, Carolina wren, chipping sparrow, and northern mockingbird.

If you are looking for ways to add a new dimension to your backyard bird-feeding program, try peanut butter. It is easy to store and use, and the birds will certainly enjoy it. In fact, the only problem you will have is stocking enough for your family *and* your feathered neighbors.

October 29, 2008

PUMPKINS—GREAT FOR HALLOWEEN AND WILDLIFE TOO

Have you noticed that pumpkins mean different things to different people? For a child, pumpkins represent jack-o'-lanterns and Halloween. Homeowners, on the other hand, consider bright-orange pumpkins to be ideal fall yard decorations. To those among us who enjoy fine food, pumpkins conjure up thoughts of pumpkin pie, stew, soup, roast pumpkin, and other delicacies. Unfortunately, few think of pumpkins as being a source of food for wildlife.

Although the name *pumpkin* is derived from the Greek word for large melon (*pepon*), early American colonists are credited with giving this large, colorful fruit this name. By the time these settlers arrived in the New World, Native Americans had been using pumpkins, a plant native to this soil, for generations in a number of ways. Both the seeds and flesh were consumed as food, and pumpkins were also cut into strips, pounded, and then woven into mats. Additionally, pumpkin seeds were even used as medicine.

Each year, far more pumpkins are raised than are ever eaten. This is because most pumpkins are used exclusively as decorations. Instead of simply tossing your used pumpkins into the trash after Halloween or Thanksgiving, why not offer them up as a post-Halloween wildlife food?

Small pumpkins can be placed around the yard for raccoons and other animals that eat fruits and vegetables. If you want to be creative, fashion a face on an old pumpkin using an assortment of fruits and vegetables, such as carrots and apples. Then sit back and see which parts of your creation prove to be favored by your wildlife neighbors. Larger pieces can be cut up into chunks and placed in secluded parts of the yard. These pieces provide food for late butterflies and other insects that dine on plant juices. Pieces of pumpkins can be mixed with slices of apples, pears, and other fruits and presented in shallow pans. Better yet, a pumpkin shell can be cut to fashion a shallow bowl in which seeds and other food offerings can be placed. At this time of the year, your fruit salad might attract American robins, northern mockingbirds, rose-breasted grosbeaks, northern cardinals, hermit thrushes, brown thrashers, or perhaps a gray catbird or two that has lingered long after its cohorts have departed for their wintering grounds in Mexico, the Caribbean, and northern Central America.

Whether you are creating a jack-o'-lantern or simply cutting up a pumpkin to make a holiday dish, don't throw away the seeds. Many birds find the pumpkin's large, off-white, flat seeds every bit as desirable as sunflower seeds. The list of birds that relish sunflower seeds includes a host of backyard favorites, including northern cardinals, Carolina chickadees, tufted titmice, white-breasted nuthatches, blue jays, dark-eyed juncos, rose-breasted grosbeaks, purple finches, mourning doves, and two introduced species—the European starling and the house sparrow.

Before pumpkin seeds are fed to birds, they should be dried. This is a simple process. Begin by removing the seeds from the stringy pulp surrounding them. Then, place them on either paper towels or a screen, and allow them to dry. They can also be dried in an oven on low heat. Place the seeds into bags, and store them in a freezer until you are ready to use them.

Pumpkin seeds will last up to three months when dried and frozen.

Whether you look at pumpkins as traditional holiday delicacies, yard ornaments, scary symbols of Halloween, or food for backyard wildlife, I think you will agree that these colorful fruits have become an integral part of the tapestry of autumn in Monroe County.

MOVING WATER ACTS LIKE A BIRD MAGNET

I f you are trying to attract your feathered neighbors to your back-yard, undoubtedly you already know that one of the easiest ways to do so is to provide them with a dependable source of water. Shallow birdbaths are often used for this purpose. They are inexpensive and easy to maintain—and the birds flock to them. What you may not realize, however, is that believe it or not, you can actually increase the numbers and variety of birds visiting your birdbath by using devices that move the water. For reasons that aren't fully understood, the combination of the sound and sight of moving water acts as a magnet for birds.

You can create this effect by simply punching a small hole in the bottom of a bucket or two-liter bottle, filling the container with water, and hanging it above a birdbath. The size of the hole regulates how fast the water leaks out of the container. As the water slowly drips from the bottle or bucket into the birdbath, it creates ripples and a methodical dripping sound. The same effect can be achieved by placing a shallow pan beneath a slowly dripping faucet or hose hung over a limb. Running a small recirculating pump in a birdbath also works well.

My favorite water mover is the mister. Misters release a fine spray of water into the air. Misters seem to work best in spots where the mist bathes the nearby foliage. The water that collects on the leaves and slowly drips into a birdbath is particularly irresistible to migrating warblers.

Another bird that is particularly fond of misters in the ruby-throated hummingbird. This tiny summer resident doesn't often bathe or drink from birdbaths. However, once a mister is up and running, these tiny aerialists make a habit of flying through the fine mist.

The key to attracting birds with a mister is finding one that emits an extremely fine mist. Most misters that are designed for home irrigation systems aren't fine enough. While birds may occasionally use them, such misters use far too much water. The best misters are designed specifically for bird use. Such devices are most often available at stores specializing in birding supplies.

The neatest device designed to attract birds to the sight and sound of running water is the wiggler. This innovative gizmo sits in the middle of a birdbath on four plastic legs. Powered by batteries, the water wiggler creates ripples on the surface of the bath by rapidly vibrating. Some models even come equipped with a recording of the sound of moving water. A switch allows you to control the volume of the recording. I must admit that I haven't tried one of these gadgets. If you do give one a try, let me know how it worked for you.

These devices seem to work best during the spring and fall songbird migrations. Since the fall migration has already begun, if you decide to try a water mover, I suggest you hop to it, or you will miss the opportunity to attract a host of migrants as they head toward their wintering grounds outside the United States.

Once you have installed a mister or other water-moving device, keep a field guide and pair of binoculars near a window that overlooks the birdbath. The reason for this is simple—these devices will help attract birds that you may never have seen before in your backyard. Migrants such as thrushes, vireos, and warblers that once flew over your yard might very well drop in for a bath and drink before resuming their epic journey. Also, don't be surprised if Carolina chickadees, cardinals, northern mockingbirds, brown thrashers, chipping sparrows, and other permanent residents begin making visits to your birdbath more often.

Regardless of the device you employ, don't forget to keep your birdbath clean. Dirty water can be every bit as dangerous to birds as dirty bird feeders. Keeping a birdbath clean is a paltry price to pay for the pleasure you receive watching the parade of fascinating birds visiting the backyard oasis you have created just outside your backdoor.

TIME FOR SPRING CLEANING

O ne of our least popular annual rituals is spring cleaning. But thoroughly cleaning the house, washing the windows, and performing all of those other tasks that make our homes more beautiful and livable are necessary evils. With this in mind, when you are preparing your list of spring-cleaning tasks, don't forget to maintain your nesting boxes. They too need a little TLC in the spring.

Too often, we are guilty of erecting a nesting box and simply forgetting about it. As a result, the box either falls into disrepair or becomes a death trap to both nesting adults and their young.

If you haven't checked your nesting box since last nesting season, a good place to start is to open it to see if it was used by any birds. Just to be on the safe side, before you put your hand into a nesting box containing an old nest, you might want to slip on a pair of surgical gloves. Hopefully you will find that it contains a nest. Since some birds are already nesting, try to determine if the nest is new. If the nest contains eggs, remember that new eggs will have a sheen and look clean. Eggs that were laid last year will appear dull. Old nests will often contain droppings, old feathers, and abandoned eggs or young. If you aren't sure whether or not you are looking at a fresh or an old nest, leave it alone, and recheck in a week or so.

A box that hasn't been checked for a number of years will sometimes contain several nests built atop one another. When this happens, the birds that use the box are forced to nest ever closer to the entrance hole. Although this might not appear to be a big deal, it actually is. This allows predators like raccoons and cats to more easily reach in and pluck out nesting birds and/or their eggs and young.

If the box doesn't contain a new nest, I recommend that you remove any old nesting material. This will help eliminate any parasites that may be lurking in the remains of the old nest. While it is impossible to rid a box of all parasites, cleaning it will keep parasites at levels where they won't pose a threat to adults or their young.

It is also a good idea to follow this up by spraying the inside of the box with a 0.5 percent pyrethrum spray.

When you remove an old nest, don't simply drop the old nesting material on the ground. Dispose of it at least fifty feet from away from the box. This will remove a host of mites, lice, and other pests while preserving valuable chalcid wasps. You might be wondering why this is important. The reason is that these wasps prey on the pupal cases of the blowfly, a serious pest on bluebirds and other nesting birds. The wasps will find their way back to the, box but the parasites won't.

Before you close the box, remove any paper wasp nests that might be attached to the underside of the top of the box. No bird likes to share a nesting cavity with these neighbors.

Next, if you haven't already done so, fasten a heavy metal entrance hole guard around the box's entrance hole. This handy device will prevent flying squirrels and woodpeckers from increasing the size of the entrance hole. This will prevent these critters from literally destroying your valuable nesting box.

Replace all rotten, warped, or cracked boards. At the same time, reset any loose nails or screws. The last thing you want to happen is to have a box fall apart when it contains nestlings or eggs.

If the box is attached to a tree, make sure it has not grown so thick that it is about to force the box off its trunk. With that in mind, leave ample space between the box and the head of the nail or lag bolt used to attach it to the tree's trunk.

Next, unless your nesting boxes are made of redwood or cedar, repaint the boxes as needed. This will greatly extend the life of the box.

Additionally, if a box was originally painted a dark color, consider repainting it with light-colored paint. The interior of a dark-colored box gets hotter than one painted a light color. While this may not be a problem for early nesters, such is not the case for bluebirds and other cavity nesters that are often still nesting during the late spring and summer. At this time of year, temperatures can rise so high in a dark-colored box standing in direct sunlight that eggs and young birds can be destroyed.

Also, don't forget to inspect the predator guard protecting the box. If the box isn't protected by guards, install one. Boxes that are unprotected by predator guards have a greater chance of being visited by rat snakes and other predators than those not equipped with these simple devices.

Last but not least, cut away any vines or branches growing within six feet of a box. Vegetation growing in close proximity to a box can be used by predators to reach the box.

When you expand your spring cleaning to include the nesting boxes on your property, you will experience the satisfaction of knowing that you helped ensure that the birds using the boxes will successfully fledge young this year.

May 12, 1999

BAT BOXES DESERVE A SECOND CHANCE

Until recently, bat boxes have had a short and unspectacular history in the United States. Since their introduction here in the 1980s, it has been estimated that only 10 percent of these original boxes were ever actually inhabited by bats. Here in the South, in all likelihood, occupation rates have probably been much lower. I don't personally know of any boxes that were used by bats in Monroe County. Today, however, newly designed bat boxes, placed in locations researchers have found to be preferred by bats, are enjoying dramatically increased occupation rates. These success rates have earned bat boxes a place in your backyard.

The newly designed boxes are larger and much slimmer than the older models. They are at least twenty-four inches tall and possess roosting chambers measuring at least twenty inches from top to bottom. These boxes should be a minimum of fourteen inches wide. These new dwellings also have open bottoms and roosting partitions varying from three-quarters of an inch to one inch apart. While bats seem to prefer boxes with open bottoms, birds, mice, and even squirrels tend to shy away from them. Since different species of bats prefer roosting crevices of varying widths, offering spaces of different widths increases the chances that a variety of bats will use a box.

The interior surfaces of any bat box must be rough. Such surfaces make it easier for bats to attach themselves to the interior of the box. Pieces of fiberglass window screening (one-eighth- to one-quarter-inch mesh) tacked or stapled to the partitions are ideally suited to providing roosting surfaces. If rough roosting surfaces are created by cutting grooves into the inside of a box, these grooves should be spaced one-quarter inch apart.

Here in the Southeast, evidence suggests that one of the reasons bat boxes have been ignored by bats is that they simply got too hot. A few things can be done to address this problem. For example, the top of the box can be insulated. In addition, ventilation slots can be placed in the front of the box, cut about one-third of the way between the bottom and top. These vents should extend across the entire front of the structure. If side vents are installed, they should be about six inches tall and wide. Last, but not least, unless a box is placed in a shady area, paint or stain boxes a light color. Surfaces treated with light-colored coatings absorb less heat than those painted or stained dark colors.

Another one of the innovations found on new boxes is a landing area immediately below the entrance. This feature can be provided by either recessing the partitions three to six inches or extending the back of the box three to six inches below the entrance.

The box needs to be constructed of either cedar or exterior-grade plywood. In addition, the structure should be held together with noncorrosive screws and nails. It is important that none of the sharp points on the fasteners extend into the interior of the box.

All joints should be either caulked or glued. This will help prevent a box from warping and keep drafts from entering the box. Bats definitely don't like drafty abodes.

Last but not least, tack a shingle to the top of the box. A box equipped with a shingle will last far longer than one without this protection.

Once you have a great bat box, whether or not it will attract bats will depend on where you mount it. Recent research has revealed that boxes most often used by bats are those located within a quarter mile or less of a river or stream or a lake three acres or larger in size and those exposed to four or more hours of sunlight daily. Some studies have found that upward of 83 percent of boxes situated in such locations were occupied.

While many homes have such a habitat, all is not lost if they don't; bats will also use boxes erected in other locations. For example, bat boxes can be attached to the sides of buildings. In fact, as a rule, such boxes are used sooner than those erected on trees. If you do attach a box to a building, placing it under an eave will protect it from the weather. In addition, try positioning the box on the east side of the building. This will expose it to the morning sun as well as the afternoon shade.

Bat houses placed on trees and poles seem to work best when poised at least fifteen to twenty feet above the ground. If given a choice, place boxes on poles instead of trees. It is much easier to place a predator guard on a pole than a tree. Such guards will help protect bats from rat snakes and other predators.

Success rates seem to be enhanced when boxes are arranged in groups of three or more. Such groupings allow bats to move from box to box depending on weather conditions. Bachelor males and females without young prefer boxes that are ten to twenty degrees Fahrenheit cooler than females with young. Avoid sites exposed to exterior lighting, air vents, streets, or prevailing winds.

If bats don't use your bat boxes immediately, don't get discouraged. It will sometimes take a year or more before bats will move in. If they are slow to respond to your welcome sign, try changing their location. Sometimes simply moving a box a few feet or pointing it in a different direction can make a box more desirable to bats.

At least sixteen species of bats make their home in Georgia. Three of these species (big brown, evening, and Mexican free-tailed) are the bats most likely to use bat boxes in the Peach State. These flying mammals can be valuable neighbors, devouring untold numbers of insects and adding to wildlife diversity around your home. A single big brown bat, for example, can devour three thousand to seven thousand insects a night.

If you are thinking about putting up a few bat boxes this year, don't procrastinate. If you erect the boxes in March and April, with a little luck, bats will be patrolling your neighborhood and devouring thousands of insects on warm summer nights this year.

With a healthy colony of bats living in your backyard, you won't need an electric bug zapper.

June 24, 2009

ORPHAN OR FLEDGLING?

Those of us lucky enough to have birds nesting around our homes eventually come across a young bird that appears to have fallen from or left its nest too soon. Invariably when this happens, we assume the bird is an orphan and will die unless we come to its rescue. In truth, in far too many cases, when we try to be a good Samaritan, we do more harm than good. With that in mind, here are a few tips that will help you do the right thing when faced with this perplexing situation.

The first thing you need to do is carefully examine the bird for injuries. If it is alert and tries to run or fly away, it probably doesn't need your help. On the other hand, if the bird is obviously injured, feels cold, suffers from insect bites, or has glazed eyes, it probably needs a helping hand. However, don't attempt to treat the bird yourself. Call the Game Management Section (478-825-6354) or the local Nongame Wildlife Conservation Program office (478-994-1438) for the name and telephone number of the closest wildlife rehabilitator trained and licensed to treat the animal.

If the bird is mostly naked or covered with down, it is a nestling that left its nest far too soon and will never survive on its own. Since it is not capable of moving very far, its nest must be close at hand. If you see a nest nearby, don't assume that the bird in your hand fell from that nest. Peek into the nest and the see if birds nestled inside are of a similar size and appearance. The last thing you want to do is drop a young cardinal into a mockingbird's nest.

If you are certain you have found the right nest, gently place the bird beside its nest mates. Don't worry about the parents' abandoning it. Contrary to popular belief, they will not abandon their youngster simply because you touched it.

After you have returned the bird to the nest, watch the nest from a discreet distance for an hour or two. If an adult bird doesn't return to the nest during that time, the bird and its nest mates are likely orphans and should be placed in the care of a licensed rehabilitator.

If the nest has been damaged, place the nestling in small box, plant pot, or basket, and set it as close to the original nest as possible. Line the makeshift nest with pine straw and not grass. Grass will retain moisture, which in turn can promote the growth of harmful bacteria and mold.

Whatever you do, don't try to raise the youngster by yourself. First of all, it is against to law to do so without a permit. Additionally, unless you are a wildlife rehabilitator, you probably don't have the knowledge or time to raise a young bird. Young birds require a special diet as well as a major commitment of time. They often require feeding several times an hour for fourteen hours a day.

If the bird is fully feathered but still sports a very short tail, it is probably a fledgling. Try as you might, it will be next to impossible to force such a bird to stay in the nest. About the best you can do is to place it in a nearby tree or shrub. This will reduce the chances that a cat, dog, or other predator will pounce on it.

When fledglings are testing their wings for the first time, their first flights aren't pretty. Such flights are often wobbly and end in a crash landing. For that reason, when birds are fledging in your backyard, it is a good idea to prevent the family dog or cat from wandering about. The last thing you want is for the bird's maiden flight to be its last.

Once a bird fledges, the parents will quickly find and feed the precocious youngster for several days. In fact, an adult was probably carefully watching you as you tried to rescue the bird.

One more thing. It is extremely important to act quickly. The longer you wait, the lower the chances that the bird will survive the ordeal.

DEER OFTEN TAKE THE BLAME
FOR "WABBITS"

If you plant a vegetable garden in Monroe County, you will invariably go out to your garden one day and find that your bush beans or other prized plants have suddenly disappeared. Invariably when this happens, we blame white-tailed deer for the damage. While in many cases they are indeed the culprits, sometimes they take the blame for a creature that tips the scales at only two to three pounds—the eastern cottontail rabbit.

Most of us have grown up with the knowledge that rabbits are fond of eating in gardens. Most children know all about Beatrix Potter's fanciful tales of Peter Rabbit's adventures in Mr. McGregor's garden. Then, of course, there are the cartoon adventures of Elmer Fudd trying to keep a pesky "wabbit" named Bugs Bunny out of his carrots.

It has been my experience that deer damage is greatest at certain times of the year. Deer seem to raid gardens most often early in the growing season and when crops are ready to be harvested.

I can't tell you how many times people have told me how uncanny it is that on the night before they are going to pick a mess of butter beans, deer descend on the garden to enjoy a hefty nighttime butterbean snack, leaving few to pick for the freezer the next morning.

Rabbits, on the other hand, are more apt to feed in your yard throughout the year. In fact, some of their worst damage occurs in the winter, when they sometimes girdle fruit trees.

While rabbits will eat a wide variety of plants, for some reason they rarely bother cucumbers, potatoes, squash, peppers, corn, or tomatoes. They will, however, eat a variety of ornamental and food plants. They seem to really like tulips when they first burst through the cold earth in the spring. They will also dine on the buds, bark, and limbs of apples, roses, plums, and pecans.

Before you can effectively solve your plant damage problem, you need to identify what animal is causing it. Often this requires being able to read the signs left behind by these nighttime marauders.

The first thing to look for is tracks. Deer tracks look like broken hearts and are upward of three to three and a half inches in length. In comparison, rabbits leave two types of tracts. The tracks made by their hind feet are three to four inches long. The forefeet leave round one- to one-and-a-half-inch impressions.

Droppings are also great clues. Rabbit droppings are typically round (one-half inch in diameter) and are often left in piles of six or more. Some say they look much like chocolate-covered raisins. Meanwhile, deer pellets are larger one-half or three-quarter inches long) and acorn or oval shaped.

Since rabbits have both top and bottom front teeth, stems they nip off are cleanly cut in two. However, since deer have front teeth on only the bottom of the mouth, the stems left on plants they have eaten will have ragged edges.

Additionally, rabbits are much smaller than deer; consequently, the damage they inflict on plants will take place within two feet of the ground. While deer damage is also found in this zone, if portions of your plants are damaged higher than this, it could have been done by Bugs Bunny but more likely a deer.

If your detective work reveals that rabbits are the perpetrators, don't worry. Although Mr. McGregor and Elmer Fudd were never able to thwart the wily efforts of Peter Cottontail and Bug Bunny, nowadays homeowners have an arsenal of effective means of dealing with these animals. One of the easiest ways to keep rabbits away from flower beds and backyard gardens is to erect a fence. Such fences need not be tall. In fact, all that is necessary is a two-foot fence made out of chicken wire with a mesh measuring one inch or less. It is important that the fence be flush with the ground. In fact, some gardeners will bury the bottom of the fence some two to three inches in the ground to ensure that rabbits don't dig under it.

If you are trying to prevent rabbits from girdling young trees and shrubs, you should consider wrapping cylinders made of quarter-inch hardware cloth around the plants. The wire should be at least twenty inches tall and positioned around the tree or shrubs being protected so that the hardware cloth is at least two inches away from the plant's trunk. Special tree wraps can also be purchased for this purpose.

A number of rabbit repellents have appeared on the market. Not all of these products live up to their hype. For that reason, I suggest you contact a wildlife biologist for the latest information regarding which are the most effective rabbit repellents.

Over the years, I have become much more willing to share my ornamental plants and vegetables with my wildlife neighbors. They don't really eat that much, and I do enjoy watching them in my yard. I'm sure Beatrix Potter would be proud of me.

PART 8

A Cornucopia

TAKING THE TIME TO WATCH

E very day, I see wildlife in my yard. Like most of you, however, I am often guilty of thinking I am too busy to catch more than a fleeting glimpse of most of the animals I see. When I tarry long enough to closely watch, however, I am often treated to some incredible sights.

Take last week, for example; while I was writing at my computer, I paused several times to watch the birds that were attracted to the feeders just outside my window. I find that such breaks are relaxing and give me the opportunity to collect my thoughts. During one of these respites, a flash of blue caught my eye. A blue jay had flown in and landed on the limb of a redbud tree just beyond the feeders.

I could tell it was carrying something; however, the bird was perched just far enough away to prevent me from making out just what it was.

Since my camera, equipped with a telephoto lens, was sitting on a tripod nearby, I focused on the blue jay and snapped off several shots. I then took a quick glimpse at the images. Boy, was I ever surprised to find that the blue jay was carrying three acorns in its formidable dark bill.

As I intently watched what the bird was going to do with its bill stuffed full of acorns, it eventually flew down to the ground and began hopping from place to place, seemingly looking for something. I said to myself, "Surely it isn't going to try to pick up a fourth acorn." I didn't have to wait long to find out what the bird had in mind.

Somehow, while holding the three acorns tightly in its bill, the blue jay chiseled out a shallow hole in the brick-hard red soil. After completing the hasty excavation, it dropped an acorn inside. Then, with a quick sweep of its bill, the bird covered its treasure and hopped to another spot. Repeating the procedure, it buried the second acorn. Moving on, the blue jay did the same with the third acorn. This time, however, after the seed was hidden, it picked up a leaf and casually flipped it over the spot where the final acorn was concealed.

After the blue jay flew off, I sat for a moment, replaying in my mind what I had just observed. I knew that each year, blue jays plant thousands of acorns across the Monroe County countryside. In fact, many of the white and other oaks that are such important sources of food for white-tailed deer, turkeys, quail, and other wildlife were planted by blue jays years ago.

In spite of the fact that I have spent countless hours in woods and fields from Canada to Florida, I had never witnessed this fascinating behavior. As I pondered over what I had just seen, I couldn't help but shake my head and smile over the fact that I witnessed this behavior from my soft seat, gazing out my office window. Oh well, what can I say?

A few days later, I was once again sitting in front of my computer when I was treated to another interesting sighting. This time, I was entertained by a steady stream of brown-headed nuthatches, Carolina chickadees, and tufted titmice flying back and forth between a nearby redbud tree and one of my feeders stocked with sunflower seeds. Each bird would fly in, snatch a seed, and then retreat to a favorite perch, crack the seed open, eat the contents, and then return for another.

For some reason, one particular brown-headed nuthatch caught my eye. After grabbing a seed, it always flew back to the same spot on a nearby tree limb. This piqued my curiosity, so I grabbed a pair of binoculars and took a closer look at the bird. With the aid of the 8-power binoculars, I could clearly see that the tiny bird was stuffing each seed into a knothole situated atop the limb. As I continued to watch, the bird made several more trips to and from my feeder.

Apparently I wasn't the only one watching the bird cache sunflower seeds in the hollow, as out of nowhere a male cardinal flew down and chased the nuthatch away. As the tiny bird flew off, the much larger cardinal began helping himself to the energy-rich seeds. Who said nature is fair?

The best deer hunter I know once told me that when he began deer hunting, he was so anxious to bag a deer that as soon as a deer came within range, he'd take a shot at it. After hunting this way for several years, he eventually became more selective. In his quest for a trophy, he began letting most of the deer that passed in front of him go about their daily routine. By so doing, he was able to learn more about the behavior of whitetails than ever before. He told me he was convinced that the knowledge he gained from watching these animals made him a better hunter.

Anybody who enjoys watching wildlife can learn from his experience. If you take the time of watch wildlife in your yard, you will invariably learn a lot about your wildlife neighbors' habits and how they interact with other animals and humans. Additionally, you will quickly discover that you don't have to travel to some far-off destination to enjoy wildlife adventures. Every day, countless intriguing wildlife dramas are played out in our backyards. If you want to enjoy seeing them, all you have to do is take the time to watch. If you do, eventually you will be treated to a story with a surprise ending.

HOW WILDLIFE COPES WITH THE HEAT

If you live in Monroe County, I don't have to tell you that it has been hot during the final weeks of spring. Temperatures have soared into the high nineties, more characteristic of August than June. While these stifling-hot temperatures have stressed each and every one of us, they have also been tough on our wildlife neighbors. Although many wild animals have quite different ways of dealing with the heat than we do, some are remarkably similar.

As soon as it gets hot, one of the first things we do is put our heavy winter clothing away and don clothes made of light, cool fabrics. Likewise, many different kinds of wildlife also "dress" for the season. Some birds, for example, are cloaked with fewer feathers in summer than winter. The American goldfinch has hundreds fewer feathers in summer than in winter. Weeks ago, local white-tailed deer shed their heavy, gray winter coats in favor of a less bulky reddish-brown summer pelage. The lighter summer coat is made of thousands fewer hairs than its winter coat. This allows air to reach the skin of the animal and permits what little sweat a deer produces to quickly evaporate, cooling the animal down. Deer will also pant to rid themselves of body heat.

During the current heat wave, most of us have dramatically altered our activities. Gardening and other yard chores are reserved for early in the morning or late in the afternoon. Our wildlife neighbors have also changed their habits. Many animals that are usually active throughout the day have also adopted a similar strategy.

Fish, such as bluegills and bass, are feeding early and late. During the hottest parts of the day, many also seek refuge beneath the banks of streams or retreat to deep water, where the water temperature is lower and dissolved oxygen is more abundant.

It can even get too hot for butterflies. When the thermometer soars above one hundred degrees Fahrenheit, many butterflies seek refuge in shady spots. At that time of the day, if you look carefully, you can sometimes spot butterflies perched in the shady foliage of trees and shrubs or on the undersides of leaves.

Often, birds will stop calling and searching for food and retreat to thick vegetation when it gets too hot. I recently ran a breeding bird survey on a very hot morning. Finding birds early in the day was a snap. However, when the day really began to heat up in mid-morning, fewer birds were seen or heard.

Reptiles and amphibians will also seek relief from the heat. Some will retreat to shelter beneath rocks and logs and even deep within burrows, where temperatures are cooler.

In hot weather, some critters like wild turkeys will scratch shallow depressions in the ground until they have exposed cool, moist soil. Then they will then plop down into these scrapes to cool off.

During the summer, youngsters and oldsters alike seek relief from torrid temperatures by taking a dip in the pool. Birds also look for shallow pools to cool down in warm weather. Bluebirds, catbirds, thrashers, chipping sparrows, tufted titmice—you name it—will regularly bathe in puddles and birdbaths during hot weather.

While our local birds don't head to the mountains to escape the heat, birds such as vultures find relief by soaring high in the sky, where temperatures are much cooler than they are closer to the ground.

The turkey vulture also has one of the most bizarre ways to keep cool—it will actually defecate on its legs and feet. The caked-on waste actually cools its legs. At the same time, the bird's acidic droppings will kill harmful bacteria living there.

While few people like to sweat, perspiring is a very efficient way to dissipate body heat. Unfortunately, for all practical purposes, many animals—from the family dog to deer and birds—sweat very little, if at all.

Bats have an interesting alternative to sweating. During hot weather, the blood vessels in this mammal's ears and membranes on its wings dilate. This greatly increases blood flow through these vessels located close to the animal's skin. This enhances the heat loss through the thin membranes. In an effort to aid this process, bats will stretch out and fan their wings.

Birds will also hold out their wings to lose heat. This technique is often employed by a list of birds that includes vultures, cormorants, and anhingas.

Birds cope with this problem in a couple of other ways too. On a hot day, if you spot a bird such as a mockingbird, brown thrasher, or chickadee with its mouth open, very likely it is panting. As the air passes out the bird's mouth, heat is lost. Over the course of a day, a panting robin can rid itself of half its metabolic heat in this manner.

Other birds such as cormorants, mourning doves, herons, owls, quail, and turkeys dissipate heat through gular fluttering. This simply means they lose heat by vibrating the skin beneath their bills.

You might be surprised to learn that as a general rule, animals with larger bodies are less bothered by the heat than smaller critters. In other words, a coyote would be less affected by torrid temperatures than the rabbit it is chasing. Think of it this way—it takes less time to heat a cup of water than it does a pan of water.

Like us, many wild animals drink more water in hot weather. White-tailed deer obtain much of the water their bodies require from the food they eat. However, when it is hot and dry as well, the water content of their foods plummets. At such times, deer will sometimes increase the amount of water they drink from three-quarters of a quart to one and a quarter quarts per day.

On the other hand, doves, which rely on surface water to meet their water needs, drink four times more water when the temperatures reach one hundred degrees Fahrenheit than when the temperature hovers around seventy degrees Fahrenheit.

Many people today can't imagine what life was like before the air conditioner. In truth, it is a fairly new invention. Back in the day, folks coped with the heat quite well. As such, even if we had no air conditioners today, both we and our wildlife neighbors would find a way to make it through the long, hot days of summer. I must admit, though, air conditioning is nice!

SURVIVING FRIGID WEATHER

The arctic weather that ushered in the new year has pushed temperatures into the teens. In response to this frigid weather, we Monroe Countians have been spending more time than usual in our cozy homes. And when we have been forced to leave the confines of our warm abodes, we have been donning heavy winter coats, hats, and gloves in an effort to ward off the cold. At best, the abnormally chilly weather has been little more than an inconvenience for most of us. Such has not been the case with our wildlife neighbors, though. To them, dealing with the extremely cold weather has been a life-or-death struggle. Fortunately, many animals are well adapted to dealing with the cold.

One way birds keep warm is by fluffing out their feathers to trap their body heat. The air between the fluffed-out feathers acts as excellent insulation. A Carolina chickadee, for example, uses an intricate network of tiny muscles to fluff some two thousand feathers that cloak its body.

Other birds like the American goldfinch will grow more feathers as winter approaches. The additional feathers provide added insulation.

Birds also keep warm by shivering. Since small birds are affected by the cold more than larger birds, they have been found to shiver almost continuously when temperatures drop below freezing. In fact, some birds such as the black-capped chickadee (a close relative of our Carolina chickadee) can actually sleep while it shivers. Shivering can keep an American goldfinch five times warmer than it would be it if weren't shivering.

Keeping warm in cold weather requires more energy just to survive. Tiny birds like hummingbirds can literally starve to death trying to stay warm on a bitterly cold night if they haven't eaten enough food to fuel their high metabolism. Birds such as the turkey vulture and mourning dove are capable of reducing their body temperature on cold nights. This allows them to conserve precious energy. A few birds, such as hummingbirds and Black-capped chickadees, carry this to the extreme. These feathered mites will actually go into torpor to survive the cold. In this condition, the birds remain motionless, and their body temperature, respiration, and heart rates plummet. For example, a hummingbird or black-capped chickadee body temperature, which normally hovers around 107 degrees Fahrenheit, may drop to 86 degrees Fahrenheit or so when in torpor.

You would think that since a bird's feet aren't protected by feathers, they would be vulnerable to cold weather. Actually, they aren't. First of all, little muscle tissue, which would be highly susceptible to the cold, is found in a bird's foot. Additionally, birds will often stand on one foot while keeping the other tucked up close to their warm bodies; when the foot that is exposed to the weather gets too cold, they will simply switch feet.

Have you ever wondered how ducks and geese can swim about in ice-cold water without damaging their legs and feet? The answer to this perplexing question is simple: they have the ability to constrict the veins found along the outside of their legs and feet. This forces blood into close proximity to the warmer blood flowing through arteries from the heart. This warms the chilly blood passing through the veins returning blood to the heart, thereby preventing damage to the leg and foot tissues.

Quail will keep warm at night by roosting in a tight circle with their wings slightly elevated. Each bird arranges itself so that it faces out. This arrangement allows the birds to more easily detect a predator coming at them from any direction. It also allows the birds to share their body heat, thereby keeping them warmer than they would be if they roosted alone.

Animals such as chipmunks and raccoons often sleep during cold winter weather. This should not be confused with hibernation, where an animal's metabolism is greatly reduced.

White-tailed deer, on the other hand, are active throughout the coldest weather. One reason they are not normally adversely affected by cold weather is that they have extremely thick winter coats. These coats are composed of two layers. The outer hairs are called guard hairs, which blanket shorter, fine, underfur hairs. Working together, the two layers of hairs act as such an excellent insulator that snow falling on a deer's back doesn't melt.

Many animals roost in thick cover or tree and manmade cavities to ward off cold weather. Chipping sparrows, cardinals, blue jays, and mourning doves, for example, will roost in dense conifers on cold nights. Meanwhile, other animals like squirrels, woodpeckers, titmice, and bluebirds will spend the night in nesting boxes and tree cavities. During extremely cold weather, birds will often retire to roosts earlier in the afternoon than they would during warmer weather.

If you want to help your wildlife neighbors through frigid weather, there are a number of things you can do. First of all, provide them with high-quality roost sites such as brush piles, dense shrubs, vines, and trees that retain their foliage throughout the winter. When possible, dead trees harboring cavities should be left standing. Also, erect nesting boxes in your yard. A variety of boxes with different-sized holes will benefit a greater variety of animals. When the weather turns cold, safe and warm nighttime roosting sites are just as important as food.

Last but not least, stock your feeders with high-energy foods such as suet and black oil sunflower seeds.

As you can see, wildlife is well adapted to survive freezing weather. However, by offering wildlife a helping hand in coping with the cold, you will help them make it through the worst that winter can throw at them. If you do, you will feel a warm glow— even during the coldest weather.

CAN LOCAL BIRDS AND PLANTS
PREDICT THE WEATHER?

I n a time when we are increasingly more dependent on technol-
ogy, many folks still look to animals and plants to predict the
weather.

If you don't think so, think back a few weeks to February 2
when the news was full of stories about Groundhog Day. The
country was waiting to see whether or not two groundhogs would
see their shadows when they ventured forth from their winter
abodes. According to legend, if General Lee here in Georgia or
Pennsylvania's Punxsutawney Phil see their shadows at noon on
this special day, we would have to suffer through another six weeks
of unpleasant winter weather.

While we'll never know how these legends got started, it is easy
to understand why people looked to nature for signs that would
forecast the weather. Weather forecasts were at first nonexistent,
and when they became available, they were often unreliable. As
such, farmers and other people that would benefit from accurate

weather forecasts relied on yearly instalments of *Farmer's Almanac* as well as animals to predict the weather.

Although groundhogs don't make their home in Monroe County, various native plants and animals are also known for their purported ability to predict the weather. Let's take a brief look at some of them.

Since birds are so highly visible, it is not surprising that they have long been used to predict the weather. One tale tells us that when a storm is on the way, birds have a tendency to fly low and gather in large flocks on utility lines and trees. Others say that sparrows are more raucous when a shower is near.

The yellow-billed cuckoo is a summer resident. These sleek birds are sometimes called rain crows or rain doves. The reason for this is that they supposedly call more when a storm is on the way.

The brilliant-red male summer tanager is also known as a weatherman. For decades, their *tucky-tuck-tuck* call has been interpreted by some to sound like is it saying "*Wet, wet, wet.*" According to this legend, when you hear the call, be on the lookout for rain.

Another bird-related folktale states that when you see a pair of crows fly by, fine weather is in store.

Yet another old-time saying goes something like this: "If the robin sings in the bush, the weather will be harsh."

Even fish and frogs have been used to predict the weather. It is sometimes said that when frogs croak louder and for longer periods of time, you should get ready for rain. Some fishermen claim that fish will leap out of the water and feed on insects when bad weather is near.

What about mammals? Can any of them—besides groundhogs—predict weather? A popular folkloric saying claims that "when a squirrel eats nuts in a tree, the weather is warm, as warm as can be."

Squirrels have also been used to forecast the severity of winter weather. Some say that when squirrel tails are thick and bushy or when they store lots of nuts, we are in for a bad winter.

A number of insects and even spiders have been used to forecast the weather. Supposedly, spiders abandon their webs, bees and butterflies stop feeding on flowers, and bees seek shelter in their hives when rain is imminent. Ants are said to raise their mounds or block the holes to their homes when rain approaches. Others claim that just before a rain, flies seem to bite more often, and crickets chirp.

The wooly bear caterpillar is perhaps the most famous weather forecaster in the insect world. We are told that you can foretell what the upcoming winter will be like by the width of the brown band that encircles its body. Supposedly, the thicker the band, the worse the winter.

Let's turn our attention to plants. According to folklore, dandelions and clover will close their petals when rain is on the way. By the same token, morning glories are said to open their flowers when the weather is fair and close them when the weather is poor.

By the same token, when a storm is approaching, tress show the undersides of their leaves.

An old poem tells us that "if the oak flowers before the ash, we shall have a splash; if the ash flowers before the oak, we shall have a soak."

Persimmon seeds have long been used to predict winter weather. If you cut a persimmon seed in half from end to end, you will see what appears to be the image of a spoon, fork, or knife. If a spoon is revealed, we can expect lots of snow. A fork foretells a mild winter with very little snow, and a knife is a sure sign that we need to prepare for a frigid, icy winter.

I hope you have enjoyed this small sampling of folktales regarding the ability of some of our local plants and animals to predict the weather. Try them out, and see if they work. I'm sure that some days they will prove more accurate than the forecasts provided by our local television and radio stations.

THE BACKYARD OLYMPICS

I f you are like me, during the past couple of weeks, you have spent far too much time with your eyes glued to the television watching the XXX Olympic Games. If such has been the case, we are not alone—the whole world has been captivated by the athletic prowess displayed by some of the world's greatest athletes. It is hard to believe that these extremely talented men and women can perform at levels that we mere mortals can only dream about.

The more I thought about it, the more I began to wonder how the fastest and strongest athletes would stack up against some of the animals that inhabit our backyards. I decided to do a little research and came up with some findings that you might find interesting.

Let's first look at running events. The fastest Olympians are capable of racing around a track at a speed of a little more than 28 miles per hour (mph). Folks like you and me are much slower—we're lucky if we can run 18 mph.

You might be surprised to learn that the American cockroach is the fastest insect that lives in our yards. This reviled insect scampers across the ground at the breakneck speed of 3.4 mph. That speed seems mighty slow until you consider that the insect is traveling at a rate of fifty body lengths per second. To put this in perspective, an Olympian moving this fast would be running 210 mph.

However, the animal that would have the best chance of winning a gold medal for running in the Monroe County Backyard Olympic Games is the red fox. This rarely seen canine can run 45 mph. However, it would take an all-out effort for a red fox to bring home the gold, as it would be closely challenged by both gray foxes and coyotes. Coyotes have been clocked running 43 mph. The gray fox, on the other hand, is a bit slower, coming in at a speed of just 42 mph.

The white-tailed deer wouldn't even win a bronze medal, as the fastest deer can attain a maximum speed of only 35 to 40 mph. The wild turkey would also fail to make the podium for the medal ceremony—it can run 30 mph for short distances only.

When it comes to the high jump, humans would lose there too. The world's best high jumpers can clear an eight-foot bar. If a gold medal were given to the backyard animal that jumps the highest in relation to its body size, the lowly flea would carry home the gold. In spite of the fact that the flea can't jump any higher than seven inches, it can jump more than eighty times its height. This would be the same as a six-foot-high jumper soaring some 488 feet (higher than one and a half football fields stacked end to end).

If the medal were awarded on the actual height reached by Monroe County's favorite game animal, the white-tailed deer would easily win. According to the US Department of Agriculture, a deer is capable of jumping fifteen feet high.

Let's move on to the long jump. The world record stands at 29.36 feet. Again, a flea, which can jump thirteen inches horizontally, or 220 times its body length, would win. The tree frog would take home the silver medal, as it can leap 150 times its body length.

This would be like a track-and-field star jumping the length of the HMS Titanic. The bronze would go to the jumping spider. It can leap 100 times its body length. If you had that ability, you could broad jump the equivalent of the length of the basketball court at the Mary Persons High School gym.

Once again, if medals were awarded for actual distance covered, at the end of the competition, the white-tailed deer would have the gold medal draped around its neck, since its longest jumps measure up to thirty feet in length.

When it comes to weight lifting, the world record for the bench press is a whopping 965 pounds. None of the critters that live in my backyard can carry anywhere near that much. The coyote is probably capable of carrying more than any other backyard visitor in the county. Coyotes can carry ten pounds; however, they can drag an animal twice its weight. As for birds, the great horned owl is the strongest bird that visits my yard. It can carry prey weighing up to nine pounds.

Some would say that the gold medal should go to the lowly ant. This tiny insect can lift fifty times its weight. If an Olympic weight lifter shared this ability, he or she could clean and jerk four tons.

Well, there you have it. I think you would agree that the athleticism displayed by our backyard wildlife is every bit as impressive as the world's best Olympic athletes.

Sadly, we will have to wait four long years before we once again have an opportunity to marvel at the performances in the next Olympics. In the meantime, all we have to do is watch the everyday activities of our wildlife neighbors to enjoy Olympic-class athletic feats performed in our very own backyards.

ANIMALS CAN PROTECT LIVESTOCK FROM PREDATORS

S ince humans first domesticated wild animals, protecting livestock from predators has been a challenge. While Georgia
livestock owners no longer have to deal with mountain lions and
wolves attacking their animals, predation can still be problem.
Today, the main predators on our sheep, goats, hogs, and cattle
are feral or free-ranging dogs and coyotes.

Over the years, farmers have employed a variety of methods to
protect their valuable livestock from wild predators. Some of the
most intriguing and effective tools at their disposal involve the use
of animals.

One of the animals most commonly employed by livestock owners to protect their stock is the dog. The use of dogs for this purpose was developed in Europe and Asia. There, the main predators
were wolves and bears. Over the centuries, a number of different
breeds have been used as guard dogs. Some of these breeds were
specifically bred to be used for this purpose.

The use of dogs to guard livestock wasn't popular in the United States until about thirty years ago. However, when word of the success of this method of protecting valuable livestock reached American livestock owners, they began experimenting with guard dogs.

Livestock growers in the West have made greater use of guard dogs than their counterparts in other parts of the country. A few of the most common breeds used to guard livestock in America are the akbash, Great Pyrenees and komondor. Through the use of dogs, some growers have been able to reduce predation by as much as 93 percent.

It doesn't seem to matter whether male, female, or neutered dogs are used. However, the best results are realized when dogs less than two months old are raised with the animals that they will eventually protect.

In recent years, increasing numbers of donkeys are being used by Georgia farmers to protect their livestock.

When a predator enters a pasture being guarded by a donkey, the donkey will greet it with loud braying and baring of teeth. If this fails to thwart the approach of the predator, the donkey will chase the animal and try to bite or kick it.

Donkeys are particularly effective when used in small open pastures. Best results are obtained when jennies and gelded jacks are used. When two or more donkeys are placed in the same pasture, they will tend to stay close to one another and aren't as effective as a single animal. Also, since all donkeys don't make great guard animals, it is a good idea to test a donkey's potential as a livestock guard before putting it on the job. The simplest way to do this is to see how the donkey responds to a dog. If the donkey shows no aggression toward dogs, chances are it won't make a good guard animal.

One final note—it typically takes a donkey at least four to six weeks to bond with the animals it is supposed to guard. Until this bonding takes place, a donkey won't be as effective a guard animal as it will be once it bonds with the animals it is supposed to protect.

Believe it or not, llamas are also being put to work as guard animals. Remarkably, only one llama is needed to guard 250 to 300 sheep. Nationwide, in 1999, 13 percent of the country's sheep ranchers were using llamas to protect their flocks.

Llamas are particularly effective against dogs and coyotes. The reason for this is that llamas seem to be naturally aggressive toward dogs.

When a coyote or dog approaches, llamas will position themselves between the predator and the flock. They will also call, chase, and kick the predator.

Recent studies have found that cattle can also be used to protect sheep and goats from coyotes. Best results are obtained when the sheep and goats are bonded with the cattle with which they share a pasture.

The bottom line is that llamas and guard dogs are more effective than donkeys, while donkeys and llamas do their best work in fenced pastures.

In conclusion, it is always better to prevent predation than to have to deal with it after it occurs. Using animals to guard livestock is a safe, economical way to deal with this perplexing and often costly problem.

October 31, 2001

WILD ANIMALS MAKE POOR PETS

With record numbers of wildlife shows flashing across our television screens, we are treated to a parade of wild animals. Sometimes they are depicted as so cuddly and cute that we are left with the belief that they would make great pets. But nothing could be further from the truth. Actually, most wild animals are dangerous, don't do well in captivity, and/or cannot be legally kept as pets.

Under Georgia law, the vast majority of our wildlife cannot be held as pets. This lengthy list includes armadillos, bats, black bears, bobcats, squirrels (fox and gray), minks, box turtles, corn snakes, alligator snapping turtles, raccoons, red and gray foxes, river otters, swamp rabbits, skunks (black or black and white), songbirds, owls, hawks, and white-tailed deer, just to name a few.

These laws are not designed to be overly restrictive on people wishing to possess native wildlife. On the contrary, they have been carefully crafted to protect both humans and wildlife. An example of this can be found in the white-tailed deer.

The vast majority of white-tailed deer that are kept as pets are taken from the wild when they are very young. Often, well-meaning folks find a deer fawn in the woods when it is only a few days old. Its large, dark, liquid eyes, seemingly fragile body, and gorgeous spotted coat make it irresistible. Since its mother is nowhere to be seen, the person finding the deer mistakenly feels that the defenseless fawn has been abandoned.

When the deer is taken home, the rescuer quickly learns that providing the fawn with the correct diet is difficult. I have personally seen people trying to feed fawns everything from corn chips to grass clippings. Often, the fawns will suffer from malnutrition or diarrhea. In one instance, I was called to the home of a couple trying to raise a young fawn in their living room. They had become concerned about the animal's health after the fawn had made several smelly, runny messes on their shag carpet.

If you are lucky enough to raise the fawn to adulthood, your problems are not over. Since the animal has lost its fear of humans, it is going to be extremely vulnerable to being shot during the deer hunting season.

If you have raised a buck, you also have to worry about your own safety. An antlered buck is an extremely dangerous animal. During the rut, a buck that has been docile can suddenly become extremely aggressive. There have been numerous cases where antlered bucks have killed or injured their keepers. I know of one instance where a photographer working for the Ohio Department of Conservation was gored to death while photographing a buck kept in a pen. Captive bucks will sometimes even kill other deer housed in the same enclosure. In one such case in Michigan, during a two-day span, a penned buck attacked a farmer, wounded a doe, and killed two other bucks.

Wild animals can also carry diseases that can infect humans. For example, when you bring young raccoons into your home, you risk exposing yourself and your family to such deadly diseases as rabies. The vaccine that protects your dog and cat from contracting rabies cannot be used on raccoons.

Another problem that people encounter when they try to domesticate wild animals is that some of these critters are often not active during the time when people want to enjoy them. Some animals, such as flying squirrels, are nocturnal. In other words, they are active at night and sleep during the day. Consequently, just when you turn off the light and try to go to sleep, these lively little animals are racing around their cage, making enough noise to rouse even the soundest sleeper.

After you have weighed the pros and cons of keeping wild animals as pets, I think you will agree that wildlife is best enjoyed in its natural surroundings. Let's keep our wildlife wild.

PART 9

Fish and Fishing

JITTERBUGGING THE NIGHT AWAY

The Jitterbug and I go back a long way. My dad introduced me to the Jitterbug when I was in my early teens. Now, before I go any further, I guess I should explain that I am not talking about the dance. The Jitterbug I am referring to is a topwater fishing lure.

In those days, we called such contraptions plugs, and no plug looked any stranger than a Jitterbug. Like most of the popular bass plugs of that day, it was big—it tipped the scales at five-eighths of an ounce, measured three inches long, and was armed with two large treble hooks. What made this lure unique was the strange metal lip attached to the front of the lure.

When retrieved, the metal lip makes an almost hypnotic gurgling sound as it wobbles through the water. In calm water, the lure leaves a trail of bubbles behind as it is reeled in. Even if you don't get a strike, it is fun just watching and listening to it as the plug tries to entice a largemouth to strike.

While I caught a few bass fishing a Jitterbug in the daytime, it wasn't until I read an article in either *Sports Afield* or *Outdoor Life*,

I can't remember which, that I learned the Jitterbug was a deadly nighttime bait. Until that time, the only night fishing I had ever done was catfishing.

Fortunately, Jitterbugging at night is both straightforward and simple. Consequently, all I had to do was make a cast and reel the lure back in. About the only thing I had to master was retrieving my lure at just the right speed. After a little practice, I found I got the most strikes when I would retrieve a Jitterbug just fast enough to produce an easy bubbly sound.

I also learned that unless I was fishing beneath a full moon, I rarely saw the top water plug throughout most of the retrieve. As a result, I heard more strikes than I saw.

For some reason, a large percentage of the bass that tried to hit a Jitterbug at night would miss it. Often I would hear a tremendous splash; however, when I tried setting the hooks into the mouth of the fish, nothing was on the end of my line but the Jitterbug. After a number of near misses, I figured out that if I continued my retrieve instead of attempting to set the hook, a hungry bass would sometimes try to strike again. Often it would finally engulf the lure on a second or third try. Then, once I felt a steady pull on the line, I would rare back and set the hook.

Back then, it seemed that every article I read about fishing Jitterbugs at night said that the best color to use was black. That left me scratching my head. I asked myself, "How in the world can a bass see a black lure on a dark night?" However, convinced that savvy night fishermen knew more about it than I did, I purchased a couple of black Jitterbugs and gave them a try. While I am sure that black Jitterbugs work great for some folks, I must confess that I have never landed a bass on one. I experienced more strikes fishing with red-and-white and frog-finish models.

What was far and away the most heart-stopping strike I ever had took place while using a model that glowed in the dark. All you had to do was shine a flashlight on the body of the plug for a minute or two. The lure would then glow for a few casts before needing recharging.

On that particular night, I was fishing with a younger friend with whom I had never fished for bass at night. After casting for about a half hour without a strike, I made a cast into the middle of a small opening guarded on both sides by tall grass. I let the plug bob on top of the water until the small waves created by the heavy lure plopping down on the dark water subsided. I then began to retrieve the lure, which emitted a soft, eerie, greenish-white glow. We idly listened as the Jitterbug gurgled its way back to our old wooden rowboat. Suddenly, the silence of the night was smashed when a lunker savagely attacked the lure. The heart-stopping splash created by the strike was so loud that it unnerved my young friend, so much so that he quickly decided he had enough of this fun and was ready to head for the shed. Unfortunately, the lunker missed the plug and, despite repeated casts, didn't try to hit the Jitterbug again.

The best places to fish were along the edges of lily pads and other cover. This required accurate casting, which in the dark proved to be no small feat. Consequently, my friends and I spent a lot of time untangling our plugs from long lily-pad stems and other weeds when we overshot our targets.

We also had to contend with level-wing casting reels that are a far cry from current models. These reels were filled with black, braided line. When you made a cast, the reel would make a strange whirring sound as the reel's handle would rapidly spin. You controlled the length of the cast with thumb pressure on the spool. This was a difficult art to master, and more often than not, unless you were really accomplished, you spent a lot of time picking out tangles of line on your reel.

In spite of all of these difficulties, nighttime bass fishing has provided some of my most exciting fishing experiences. Sitting in a boat in the dark beneath a sky festooned with thousands of bright stars, idly talking with a good friend while listening to the sounds made by insects and other denizens of the night, make for some memorable times on the water.

I must admit I haven't fished for bass at night very often in recent years. Like most, when the hot sun goes down, I succumb to the temptation of sitting in my easy chair in my air-conditioned home. This leaves me wondering why I don't make the effort to pursue an activity that is so much fun. I'll tell you what—let's both make a promise to go night fishing for bass before the end of the summer. Additionally, we need to make a point of carrying a youngster or two along with us. Seeing them enjoy a night of Jitterbugging is something we won't forget, even if we don't catch a fish.

June 26, 2002

DO RELEASED BASS LIVE TO FIGHT ANOTHER DAY?

I t is late afternoon. A lone fisherman casts a frog finish jitter-bug toward a dead limb protruding from the placid surface of a Monroe County farm pond. The lure lands noisily on the dark surface of the pond within a foot of the gray, weathered limb. The fisherman lets the ripples created by the plug hitting the water dissipate before slowly reeling the lure back toward the boat. As the Jitterbug slowly makes its way away from the limb, it methodically rocks back and forth, generating a comforting gur-gling sound. Suddenly, a bass erupts from the water and engulfs the lure. The fisherman sets the hooks, and the battle is on. After a spirited fight, the proud fisherman grasps the lower jaw of the two-pound bass and lifts it from the water. After unhook-ing the feisty largemouth, he briefly admires his catch before easing the fish back into the water in hopes that it will live to fight another day. Will it?

That question has perplexed generations of fishermen and fishery biologists alike. A study conducted in Texas has shed some light on this nagging question.

The research project was conducted by two Texas Parks and Wildlife Fisheries biologists at Lake Umphrey, a thirty-three-acre reservoir located in east Texas. The anglers selected to catch the fish for the study were required to use lures with treble hooks (Rebel Pop-R, Rat-L-Trap, and Bomber 7A), as well as 3/0 single hooks (plastic worms fished "Carolina rigged" and live carp). The fishermen fished on two separate days during a twenty-eight-day period. During these two events, anglers caught thirty largemouth bass with each type of bait.

When a fish was caught, records were made of the length of the fish, the type of bait it was caught on, where it was hooked, and whether or not it was bleeding. Bass that were hooked in the lip, tongue, roof of the mouth, or jaw were considered hooked in the gill. Those that were hooked behind the tongue or in the esophagus were labeled as hooked in the throat. Those that were hooked in more than one location were classified as hooked in the place that was considered the most severe.

Each fish was then tagged and placed in a live well until it was later transferred to a large holding cage. Each fish placed in the cage was checked after remaining in the cage for three days.

The biologists found that about one out of five (22 percent) of the fish released in the holding pen died within three days of capture. Interestingly, mortality didn't differ significantly between fish caught with live or artificial baits. However, the data suggests that the type of bait used did impact where fish were hooked.

For example, the fishery biologists discovered that fish caught on baits equipped with treble hooks were less likely to be hooked in the throat. It is thought this is due to the fact that fishermen using lures with single hooks, such as plastic worms and live bait, wait longer to set the hook than they do treble-hook lures.

The study found that where a fish is hooked has a tremendous impact on mortality. During the study, 48 percent of the fish hooked in the throat died within three days of capture. In comparison, only 20 percent of those hooked in the mouth and 17 percent of the fish hooked in the gill succumbed in three days.

The researchers also noted that 47 percent of the fish that were bleeding when released into the holding pen died within three days of their capture. Only one percent of the bass hooked in the mouth bled as compared to 50 percent of those hooked in the gill and 48 percent hooked in the throat.

Another interesting finding was that the mortality of bass caught with treble hooks declined with the size of the fish. In other words, larger bass taken with treble hooks had a greater chance of surviving capture than small bass. No correlation was detected between mortality and the size largemouth caught on other types of baits.

In conclusion, the study demonstrated that most largemouth bass that are released after being caught do survive. The research study also shows that catch-and-release fishing appears to be a sound practice. However, anglers should take precautions to carefully remove hooks from fish and return them to the water as soon as possible.

October 3, 2003

THE CREEK TIGER

During the first weekend of fall, I renewed my acquaintance with one of Monroe County's most voracious predators. I'm not talking about the coyote, copperhead, red-tailed hawk, or shrew. While all of these animals are indeed highly effective carnivores, this hunter is the redfin pickerel. In its watery home, this fish is indeed the top predator.

One of the things I enjoy most in autumn is the fact that dry weather allows our creeks and rivers to become as gin-clear as a north Georgia trout stream. Consequently, during this special time of year, I often stop on rural byways where slow-moving, meandering creeks pass under the roadbed and peer into the sparkling water like a prospector hoping to spot a shiny gold nugget. Unlike a prospector, the treasure that I hope to discover isn't precious metal. I am searching for living gems—brightly colored fish, crayfish, and aquatic insects that cannot be seen when the water is muddy.

I made my latest find in a shaded pool below a culvert on the Rum Creek Wildlife Management Area. I had stopped to inventory butterflies such as Carolina and gemmed satyrs, least skippers, gulf fritillaries, and sleepy oranges.

The stream that flowed under the road at this spot was so small that I gave it little notice as I scanned the nearby vegetation for butterflies. As I watched a drab Carolina satyr fly over the stream, my eyes spotted the dark form of a fish lying suspended a few inches below the surface of the water. Looking much like a tiny submarine, the fish's long, slim shape was unmistakable—it was a redfin pickerel.

Immediately, I asked myself the question, "What in the world is it doing here?" During the drought that gripped Monroe County for more than half a decade, countless small streams dried up, killing the aquatic animals that lived in their waters. I have often wondered how long it will take for fish to repopulate these creeks. Looking at this six-inch fish, I wondered if it had survived the drought in this small, deep, shaded pool or if it had moved up into the stream from Lake Juliette.

The redfin pickerel is a member of the pike family. The only other member of this family that is native to Georgia is the chain pickerel. All members of the pike family are torpedo shaped and sport long, duck-like snouts. Their mouths are full of sharp teeth that enable them to hang on to prey.

The largest member of this family of predators is the muskellunge; it can reach six or more feet in length. At the other end of the spectrum, the redfin pickerel is the smallest pike, averaging fifteen inches.

Locally, a redfin that reaches a foot in length is a big fish. The world-record redfin was caught in North Carolina and tipped the scales at two pounds, four ounces. In comparison, a large chain pickerel can measure fifty inches long. The world-record chain pickerel was landed in Homerville, Georgia, and weighed nine pounds, six ounces.

What this fish lacks in size, it makes up for in ferocity. The redfin eats mainly fish, but it will also consume aquatic insects and other aquatic life. Remarkably, it can eat a fish almost its own size. Once captured, its prey is swallowed head first.

The redfin pickerel ranges throughout the state; however, in Georgia it is most abundant in the coastal plain. It does best in slow-moving, clear creeks, swamp ponds, and the shallow waters of lakes. Here, it prefers to lie in wait within aquatic vegetation, always ready to ambush any prey that happens to swim by.

Redfin pickerel can live up to eight years. Females tend to live longer than males.

The redfin pickerel is a great game fish, particularly when taken on ultralight fishing tackle. Redfins can be caught using live minnows, spinner baits, spoons, or plugs. Veteran redfin pickerel angler Jerry Payne told me that a small red-and-white spoon is one of the best redfin pickerel lures on the market. According to Jerry, these small game fish can also be caught on something as simple as a piece of red ribbon attached to a hook. Regardless of the lure used, redfin pickerel strike with abandon and fight hard.

I know a fellow who grew up along the fringes of the Okefenokee Swamp. According to him, folks in that part of the world used to catch redfins at night by lighting a lantern and placing it in a small boat anchored in a small creek. Attracted by the light, supposedly the redfins would actually jump into the boat.

The reason most local anglers rarely hook a redfin pickerel is that these fish are most abundant in the county's smaller creeks, and such waters are rarely fished. Their narrow tree- and shrub-lined channels make casting difficult and the use of a boat often impossible. Consequently, the majority of Monroe County anglers opt to fish reservoirs, the Ocmulgee River, and farm ponds.

While redfin pickerel are delicious, most fishermen release these game fish as they are extremely bony.

If you happen to hook a redfin pickerel on light tackle, I am sure it won't take you long to agree that this slim predator deserves the nickname—the creek tiger.

EPILOGUE

When I began writing Monroe County Outdoors it was my hope the column would heighten the awareness and enjoyment of the vast array of plants and animals that live in Monroe County.

In the beginning, I focused on writing about charismatic species known to everyone such as mourning doves, white-tailed deer, the flowering dogwood, mockingbirds, cardinals, wood ducks, and wild turkeys. As I researched and wrote these weekly columns, I soon found my fascination with wildlife and plants expand to include *all* of the wild plants and animals living in the county. This interest prompted me to begin writing stories about lesser known wildlife and plants like the strawberry bush, robber flies, and Queen Anne's lace.

Remarkably, many of these plants and animals are often hiding in plain sight—living in backyards and roadside shoulders. Although we see them every day, we rarely honor them with even a fleeting glance. In spite of our indifference, they are integral parts of the colorful and complex of tapestry of the natural world around us. Also, regardless of how small or unremarkable they may appear, when we take the time to learn about them, we quickly learn that many are just as fascinating as those plants and wildlife that share center stage in the pageant of life.

When I broadened the range of topics covered in my column, I was concerned the readers of *The Monroe County Reporter* would not embrace such a dramatic change. Looking back over the past quarter century, I now wonder why I was initially so concerned about this decision. Over the years, countless people have told me that they enjoy reading about little known plants and animals too. Like me, they are now noticing wild pollinators converging on redbud trees in the spring, peering into the waters of the streams that snake their way through the county in hopes of spotting a redfin pickerel, and keeping a journal of the comings and goings of the birds and other creatures seen in their backyards.

I hope that those of you that have read the column over the years have enjoyed this journey of discovery as much as I have. For those of you that are reading these columns for the first time, I want to extend an invitation to join me on future treks through Monroe County's outdoors.

ABOUT THE AUTHOR

Terry is a retired wildlife biologist. During his thirty-five year career with the Georgia Wildlife Resources Division, he was engaged in research, surveys, habitat management, and promoting wildlife-based recreation. His career culminated serving as the first program manager of the Nongame-Endangered Wildlife Program. During this time he initiated the Acres for Wildlife and Community Wildlife Projects, and coordinated the development of Georgia's two birding trails.

Terry is a prolific writer. This is his second book. He also writes a weekly column for the Monroe County Reporter, a blog (backyardwildlifeconnection.com), and a monthly column for the Georgia Nongame Conservation Section's newsletter.

His endeavors have earned him more than sixty awards for writing, wildlife photography, and conservation.

Terry makes numerous speaking engagements, bands hummingbirds, volunteers for the Nongame Wildlife Conservation Section, and serves as Executive Director of TERN (The Environmental Resources Network).